PHalarope Books

PHalarope Books are designed specifically for the amateur naturalist. These volumes represent excellence in natural history publishing. Each book in the PHalarope series is based on a nature course or program at the college or adult education level or is sponsored by a museum or nature center. Each PHalarope Book reflects the author's teaching ability as well as writing ability.

BOOKS IN THE SERIES:

The Amateur Naturalist's Diary
Vinson Brown

The Amateur Naturalist's Handbook
Vinson Brown

The Curious Naturalist
John Mitchell and the
Massachusetts Audubon Society

Nature Drawing: A Tool for Learning
Clare Walker Leslie

The Wildlife Observer's Guidebook
Charles E. Roth, Massachusetts Audubon Society

Suburban Wildlife
Richard Headstrom

Nature in the Northwest
Susan Schwartz

At the Sea's Edge
William T. Fox

WOOD NOTES

A Companion and Guide
for Birdwatchers

Richard H. Wood

A SPECTRUM BOOK

Prentice-Hall, Inc., Englewood Cliffs, New Jersey 07632

Library of Congress Cataloging in Publication Data

WOOD, RICHARD H. (Richard Harvey), 1908–
Wood notes.

(PHalarope Books)
"A Spectrum Book."
Bibliography: p.
Includes index.
1. Bird watching. I. Title.
QL677.5.W66 1984   598'.07'2347   84-2061
ISBN-0-13-962580-1
ISBN-0-13-962572-0 (pbk.)

This book is available at a special discount when ordered
in bulk quantities. Contact Prentice-Hall, Inc., General
Publishing Division, Special Sales, Englewood Cliffs, N.J. 07632.

Editorial/production supervision by Norma G. Ledbetter
Manufacturing buyer: Doreen Cavallo
Cover design by Hal Siegel

10 9 8 7 6 5 4 3 2 1

ISBN 0-13-962580-1

IBN 0-13-962572-0 {PBK.}

PRENTICE-HALL INTERNATIONAL, INC., *London*
PRENTICE-HALL OF AUSTRALIA PTY. LIMITED, *Sydney*
PRENTICE-HALL CANADA INC., *Toronto*
PRENTICE-HALL OF INDIA PRIVATE LIMITED, *New Delhi*
PRENTICE-HALL OF JAPAN, INC., *Tokyo*
PRENTICE-HALL OF SOUTHEAST ASIA PTE. LTD., *Singapore*
WHITEHALL BOOKS LIMITED, *Wellington, New Zealand*
EDITORA PRENTICE-HALL DO BRASIL LTDA., *Rio de Janeiro*

This book is dedicated to several people. The first and most important is my wife, Frannie, who has heard so many times, without ever threatening to divorce me, "Just a minute, dear, I want to finish just one more paragraph."

Next come George and Mildred Moreland, distinguished librarians and long-time friends, who served as important "builder-uppers" during the writing of this book, indicating that they thought its contents were worth reading. They also suggested its title, *Wood Notes*.

Finally, there is "Peanuts" Carlton, with whom I took bird walks some sixty years ago in Wooster, Ohio. We used to get up early to walk out to Highland Park, about a mile away, to see the warblers when they were passing through in the spring. This did not interfere with our ball games, for we would set out no later than 5:00 A.M. I have lost touch with "Peanuts" (his given name was Bradford). If anyone knows his whereabouts, I would greatly appreciate receiving news about him.

Contents

Foreword

For years, Richard Wood has been a valued volunteer leader of bird walks at the 535 acre research reserve of the Stony Brook-Millstone Watersheds Association. He is easily spotted from a distance by the company he keeps . . . typically a group of school children from the area where rapt attention is divided between an animated Dick Wood and the feathered object of his talk. Through his knowledge and enthusiasm about birds, Dick Wood has developed a Pied Piper magnetism that makes it difficult for folks young and old to miss his trail hikes or meadow walks.

In a hurried and complex world, Dick Wood gives us a refreshing glimpse of something that is all too easy to lose, an intimate encounter with the natural world. For him, birds are exciting as much for the sounds they make as for the plumage they wear. His insights into the natural history of birds (including the origin of their names), adds a touch of lore about each species that is likely to linger on long after the particular coloration of tail feathers or primaries has been forgotten.

It is the special attention Dick gives to the behavior of birds and the peculiarities of their habitat that distinguishes him from other amateur bird watchers and "life listers." The publication of his own book will give the uninitiated a glimpse of the magic he creates. Those of us who know him, will now have a chance to "walk" with Dick Wood more frequently.

James T. Gaffney, Executive Director
Stony Brook-Millstone Watersheds Assoc.
Pennington, New Jersey

Preface

A number of excellent general bird guides are available. These include Roger Tory Peterson's *Field Guides,* found practically everywhere that birders are found, along with *A Guide to Field Identification of Birds,* by Robbins, Bruun, and Zim. More extensive bird books have been put out by the National Geographic Society, the Audubon Society, and many others. *Wood Notes,* however, is not a bird guide, and its coverage is not extensive, for it deals with only a limited number of birds. Furthermore, I am not a professional ornithologist (I received my Ph.D. in labor economics some years ago). I have not pursued birds in the Galápagos Islands, in the Arctic, Antarctic, or in Australia. However, I *am* called on occasionally to lead bird walks in the area in which I live—Princeton, New Jersey.

I have, in fact, kept a lively interest in birds since I was "waist high" to my dad. This book, therefore, might be considered as my second childhood coming to the fore.

Wood Notes has two major parts. The first of these contains my thoughts about birding in general. For example, what is the proper place for bird identification, relative to a more leisurely and deeper savoring of the mysteries and glories of each bird one sees? Also exam-

ined are the advantages of keeping a diary of all sorts
of natural events. The mysteries of bird migration, the
different dispositions of various species, and the reasons birds sing are also explored.

The second part deals with some of the more common species of birds found along the Eastern Seaboard
as well as other areas. These comments are based on
my personal experiences and aim to summarize the appearance, notes, and behavior of each bird. In the process, I attempt to relate the behavior of these birds,
when feasible, to ourselves and to human behavior.

It has been fun to do this, and I hope that these
Notes will provide fun for birdwatchers regardless of
locale, and that they will help them more fully appreciate the psalmist's observation:

The heavens declare the glory of God;
and the firmament sheweth his handy work.
                                        (*Psalm 19:1*)

May 20 —
Everything is
beginning — Found
ovenbird scampering off
nest feigning injury —
five brown-
speckled eggs
inside —
observed bird
return to nest

ground pine

Carol Decker

Nest dome shape -
open in front, pine needles,
moss & grasses.

On
Preserving a Sense
of Wonder

April 20—
Red maple buds
have burst into flowers and edge
the tree like red lace — all the
birds are singing — seem to see them now
in sets of two — Baby sparrows peeping in
Can hear the cry the barn.
of the red-tailed
hawks circling
above —
Bloodroot blooming in
the woods —
Nature's
Artwork!

Carol Decker

Many of us are subject to the tendency, as we get into the study of nature, to place our main emphasis on identifying and making long lists of what we see and hear, rather than on the deep enjoyment of each new sight or sound. This appears to be especially true of "birders," many of whom go dashing about mainly concerned with seeing as many birds as they can in the shortest possible time. Is it really of such overriding importance that the list of birds we identify be longer than that of anybody else on the same day? Or is this just another way of "winning the game" or showing off, which most of us love to do? Would Audubon's magnificent bird paintings be so magical if he had not paused to savor fully what he saw?

This basic question about how we should approach nature is raised by many respected observers. For example, Walt Whitman, in his *Specimen Days: Birds—and a Caution,* puts it this way:

> You must not know too much, or be too precise or scientific about birds and trees and flowers . . . ; a certain free margin, and even vagueness—perhaps ignorance, credulity—helps your enjoyment of these things.[1] . .

And Carl Bode, in *The Best of Thoreau's Journals,* commented this way:

> Sometimes, as Thoreau grew older, he observed too mechanically. He became in a sense scientific. He gradually learned the names for things—and used them. The names, all too often in Latin, substituted for the felt reality. . . . He himself realized that he was watching too

narrowly and categorically. "I fear that the character of my knowledge is from year to year becoming more distinct and scientific," he wrote in August 1851. And one day in September of the next year he scolded himself, "I must walk more with free senses."[2]

Edwin Way Teale, in his *Wandering Through Winter*, adds these comments along the same line:

> In later years we learn the names of things that long ago we saw and wondered at. We catalogue them in our minds. And some of the freshness fades away. Deservedly, the pursuit of factual knowledge holds a high place. Knowing the wild flowers, naming all the birds without a gun, these are admirable attainments. But there is always a residue of sadness when we learn the name and lose the wonder of the living thing itself.[3]

May all of us ponder such thoughts and linger just a bit when we hear the next white-throated sparrow or hermit thrush. Perhaps one of my young nephews said it best of all. On seeing the first morning glory of the season, his comment was, "Mommy! Look! Hooray for God!"

February—19

Slate-colored junco
eating seeds under the bird
feeder that drop on the ground—
small sized bird, makes chipping note.

forked tail

upper parts
dark grey →

pinkish-white
bill

outer tail
feathers
white

Belly
white

Carol Decker

Having inveighed against the practice indulged in by all too many birders nowadays—that of dashing about identifying birds merely for the purpose of adding to their lists without pausing really to enjoy them—let us quickly add that there are still good reasons for being able to identify birds.

For one thing, there are practical reasons for being able to distinguish birds and to count them. One important reason is in order to find out what we are doing to our environment, since this may affect all our lives. Are ospreys disappearing from the scene? If so, why, and what, if anything, should be done about it? Perhaps the increased use of pesticides is polluting our waters. If not checked, this may be poisoning all of us, along with the ospreys.

Furthermore, it is just good fun to be able to recognize familiar birds and to make the acquaintance of new ones. Also, it adds to our pleasure to be able to compare notes with other birders concerning which birds may be seen in a given vicinity from time to time.

It would seem worthwhile, therefore, to develop a method for identifying birds, so that we may be able to tell one from another. Just as in preparing for a shopping expedition or in packing for a trip, there is nothing like having a good checklist to make sure that nothing is forgotten.

Checklists useful in bird identification may include both negative and positive items. The "negative" side aims to eliminate certain species from consideration, as is done when "keys" are used in botany to identify trees: If the conifer has five needles in a bundle, it

is not a spruce. Similarly, if the bird you seek to identify is large and dark in color and is soaring quietly
high in the heavens, it will not be found among the
warblers. If it is small, highly colored, and singing lus-
tily as it pursues insects in a flowering apple tree in
April, it is not a bird of prey. Such tests generally are
used subconsciously by the experienced birder.

The "positive" side of bird identification also
tends to come fairly naturally to those who have been
at it for some time. One of the real breakthroughs
along these lines is the "Peterson system" used in
Roger Tory Peterson's field guides to the birds. On the
picture of each bird, lines are drawn to those things in
the bird's appearance that are especially helpful in its
identification. For example, a line is drawn to the red
tail of the hermit thrush.[4]

In identifying birds, at least five things should be
noted:

1. *Where did you see it?* In the deep woods? In a field?
At the sea shore?

2. *When did you see it?* In the winter? In the spring?
In midsummer?

3. *What did it look like?* How big was it? (It is helpful
here to compare its size with well-known birds like
robins, crows, or chickadees.) Was it dumpy or long in
shape? Was its tail long, short, or forked? Did it have a
crest? What was the shape of its bill? Were its legs long
or short? What colors did it display? (Peterson's system
is most helpful here in calling attention to shoulder
patches, breast spots, eye stripes, and so forth.)

4. *What sounds did it make?* Can you imitate its
notes and calls? Were they loud or soft, musical or

harsh? What were their pitch and rhythm? Did the bird whistle or warble?

5. *How did it behave?* Did it appear nervous and jumpy? Did it raise and lower its tail? Was it bold or shy? Did it climb tree trunks? Was it on the ground, and did it walk, hop, or run? Did it beat its wings rapidly or soar when it flew? Did it fly in a straight line or in a roller-coaster fashion? Did it sing during flight? What was it feeding on?

This is quite a long list of things to check on. To make it appear less formidable, let us apply it to two examples, noting that one or two rather obvious characteristics will usually identify a bird.

Example One

At the bird feeder in midwinter you see a bird about the shape and size of a sparrow. It feeds mostly on the ground. It has a slightly forked tail and displays white outer tail feathers as it flits about. Its bill is whitish. Its upper parts are dark gray, and its belly is white. The only sound it makes is an occasional light musical chip. (It does have a trill something like that of a chipping sparrow, heard especially in its Northern summer nesting grounds.)

You're right, it's a slate-colored junco.

Example Two

First of all, in the spring you hear coming from some bushes in the garden quite a jumble of notes and calls of various qualities: harsh as well as sweet, with a few "mews" thrown in. As you look, you see a largely grayish bird, slightly smaller than a robin, with a black top on its head, clearly curious about what you are doing as you approach it.

Right again, it's a catbird.

Notes taken on your observations under the five major headings as suggested above may be used as you search through the bird guides, listen to recordings of bird songs, or ask experienced birders to help you identify that mysterious stranger. Furthermore, it is remarkable how failure to follow such a checklist will often find experienced birders out in the field again, trying to see that critical eye stripe or face patch they failed to look for the first time around.

On
Keeping a Diary
of Natural Events

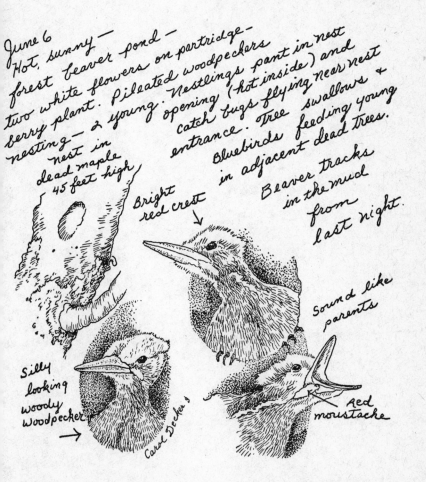

June 6
Hot, sunny —
forest beaver pond —
two white flowers on partridge-
berry plant. Pileated woodpeckers
nesting — 2 young. Nestlings pant in nest
opening (hot inside) and
nest in catch bugs flying near nest
dead maple entrance. Tree swallows &
45 feet high Bluebirds feeding young
in adjacent dead trees.

Bright
red crest

Beaver tracks
in the mud
from
last night.

Sound like
parents

Silly
looking
woody
Woodpecker

Carol Decker

Red
moustache

You do not need to be a Thomas Jefferson or a George Washington to find fun and even profit in keeping a record of the goings-on in nature about you. True, it is unlikely that posterity will dote sufficiently on every mark you make on paper to publish all you write down.

Nevertheless, keeping a journal of natural events can increase your enjoyment of spring by helping you anticipate when the first roses may appear or when you may hear the first wood thrush. It can also help you decide when and how much to water the garden and when to plant your peas to avoid having them ready for the table when you are away on vacation.

Too busy, are you? Thomas Jefferson, in spite of his many other activities, usually found time to keep a meticulous record of events taking place on his plantations when he was in Monticello for any length of time. In his preface to *Thomas Jefferson's Garden Book,* annotator E. M. Betts notes:

> He [Jefferson] was possessed of a love of nature so intense that his observant eye caught almost every passing change in it. And whatever he saw rarely escaped being recorded. So we know when the first purple hyacinth blooms in the spring, when peas are up, when they blossom and pod, and when they are ready for the table.[5]

Natural events of many sorts were usually noted in Jefferson's *Garden Book* or his *Farm Book,* and sometimes in his other memoranda or letters, and such observations often provided the foundations for his numerous experiments and conclusions about how to improve the results of agricultural activities on his own lands as well as in other parts of the world.

In a letter to Charles W. Peale in 1811, Jefferson wrote:

> No occupation is so delightful to me as the culture of the earth, and no culture comparable to that of the garden. . . . But though an old man, I am but a young gardener.[6]

His youthful enthusiasm is clearly evident in the voluminous notes he kept.

Washington and Jefferson, though differing on many public questions, were both farmers at heart as well as in their activities, at least at those times when they were able to repair to their beloved retreats of Mount Vernon or Monticello. They corresponded with each other, comparing notes on the agricultural practices and experiments they were conducting.

While Washington appeared to be somewhat less motivated by exuberant enthusiasm than Jefferson, nevertheless he clearly enjoyed his association with nature, as is shown in his letter to Arthur Young in 1788:

> The more I am acquainted with agricultural affairs, the better I am pleased with them; insomuch that I can no where find so great satisfaction as in those innocent and useful pursuits. In indulging these feelings, I am led to reflect how much more delightful to an undebauched mind is the task of making improvements on the earth than all the vain glory which can be

acquired by ravaging it by the most uninterrupted career of conquests.[7]

One indication of Washington's intense interest in agriculture is the diary he kept for many years. In commenting on this diary, Paul Haworth, in his book *George Washington,* noted:

> He called it . . . where and how my time is spent. In it he entered the happenings of the day, his agricultural and other experiments . . . and also a detailed account of the weather.[8]

In addition, as in the case of Jefferson, Washington's letters provide an even more interesting view of the importance their author attached to the natural events taking place about him.

While few of us are engaged in farming large plantations as were Washington and Jefferson, the forces of nature condition our lives in many ways, whatever we do. It would seem reasonable, then, for us to make our peace with these forces, learning to understand, enjoy, and ally ourselves with them whenever possible and as best we can. And to the extent that we write down the things we see, hear, smell, and taste, we are that much more likely to feel and understand what is going on around us, because we then become more a part of the events we record.

Why not give it a try?

The Music
of the Birds

March 20 —
Raining, new
spring smell to the air.
Song sparrow so vocal
today, sounds like auditions for
a much wanted singing part.
Cardinal singing at tops of trees — Carolina
wren & bluejays heard —
Announcements are being
made — the seasons
are changing.

carol Decker

Since a great many people seem to enjoy hearing birds sing, it is astonishing how few are able to tell their songs apart. It is not uncommon to find those who are capable of identifying a certain number of birds by their looks, especially with so many bird feeders around and with quite a few enthusiasts now involved with "bird counts" at various times of the year. Yet only a relatively few bird watchers appear to be equally skilled as "bird listeners," so that they can, for example, distinguish between the notes even of such common species as robins, Baltimore orioles, catbirds, and cardinals. As a result, it seems to me that some of the loveliest music of nature passes by most people without their fully enjoying it.

It is possible, of course, to get much pleasure from just hearing birds sing without identifying the singer (many people appear to enjoy the melody of the wood thrush, some even knowing it is "a thrush" of some sort). Yet there is much depth added to one's enjoyment by being able to associate the beauty of color and song as one becomes better acquainted with the different species. Why? The best answer is: Try it and see for yourself.

Assuming one agrees and wants to learn to identify birds by their songs as well as by their looks, how may this be done? There are several ways of doing this, including:

1. Go out with someone who knows how to identify birds both by their looks and their notes, and who can relate the two for you—but who knows enough not to try to teach you ten all at once.

2. Get recordings of bird songs, such as those put out by the Laboratory of Ornithology of Cornell University. As you listen to these records, look at the picture of each bird in a good bird guide, for example, *A Field Guide to the Birds East of the Rockies* by Roger Tory Peterson.[9]

3. Go out by yourself, again with a good bird guide, and look and listen.

The would-be bird listener will encounter two obstacles as the attempt is made to identify the singer. These are not insuperable, but it is well to mention them, so that they do not result in unexpected discouragement.

The first and by far the more important of these two obstacles is that many species have a considerable variety of songs and call notes. Many people know this about mockingbirds, but it is astonishing how hard it is, at first, to predict just what will be heard from other common species, such as chickadees, catbirds, and even robins.

The second obstacle is that individual members of certain species quite often add their individual variations to the song one comes to expect from that species. For example, there is a common quality in the song of the song sparrow; however, we have one near our house that we call the "OGPU" song sparrow, because most of his songs end with the phrase "pedrewski secret," which I have not heard from any other song sparrow. (OGPU is the former name of the Soviet secret police.)

Birds have many competitors for top place in musical loveliness. However, the beauty of song and singer are rarely so exquisitely combined as they are in the Baltimore oriole, the indigo bunting, or the gold finch in full throat.

October 31 – Mockingbird has declared
possession of the bittersweet vines. He jumps,
screams, dives & chases all intruders –
Reminds me of a very spoiled
child – but then he's looking
at a very cold winter –

and just
providing....

Carol Decker

From my observations at our bird feeder on the northern outskirts of Princeton Township, New Jersey, birds of different species display dispositions of astonishing variety. The behavior of our visitors at the feeder seems to place them in the following quite different categories:

1. Bullies—those who push others around and can't seem to stand any other birds feeding near them. Included in this group are mockingbirds, starlings, and song sparrows. The arrival of a blue jay is an event of such physical magnitude, of course, that others tend to clear out, especially the smaller species. However, the blue jay does not seem to have much of a chip on his shoulder once he has landed.

2. At the other end of the scale from the bullies are those who appear to want peace at any price. Field sparrows are good examples of this pacifist type. Not only do they have a timid look about them, but they appear so anxious to avoid conflict that they generally fly off on the approach of any other bird, without any argument.

Perhaps a subgroup should be included under the timid type—those who not only want to avoid trouble, but who always seem to be expecting the worst. Especially jumpy are the woodpeckers. Just watch a downy woodpecker furtively peeking around in every direction between pecks at your suet.

3. Fortunately, perhaps, the largest number of species fall in between these extremes, appearing to lack either excessive aggressiveness or timidity. These

might be called the "live-and-let-live" type. This group would include the chickadees (they'll dine and talk with anybody), tufted titmice, slate-colored juncos, and white-throated sparrows. They come back quickly after the bullies have left.

Some species in this in-between group have additional characteristics of being especially bouncy, inquisitive, and even nosey, but not offensively so. Chickadees, again, are outstanding examples of this type as are catbirds, although the latter rarely eat at our feeder. Nothing daunts the species in this group from exploring everything in their surroundings and appearing always to be questioning everything they see.

The behavior of birds tends to vary, of course, in situations other than at a feeder. For example, otherwise timid parents may adopt more belligerent characteristics when they are defending their nests or their young. This is not unlike the variation in behavior of those in our own species, *homo sapiens,* in different situations. One may find "cocktail party" chickadees in the midst of those they consider friends and equals, but who become timid as field sparrows before the "boss" or "mockers" determined to intimidate all "lesser folk" who may come their way

Can Spring
Be Far Behind?

March 5 —
The back of winter
is broken — Freeze loosening
on edges of lakes and ponds — Redwings
displaying "red shoulders" and calling,
"kong-ka-ree, spring is coming, find a home."
Skunk cabbage and violets up —

chipmunk
out of its bed —
trailing arbutus
blooming — smells
wonderful.

← bright red

As I am writing this, it's late March, and spring in Princeton seems to be standing on tiptoe, looking warily at the year ahead, as well it might.

Winter's footprints are still all around: bits of ice hiding here and there, wet fields, and muddy country lanes. But expectancy, hope, and faith are in the air, however chilly it may be.

Some of the hardiest adventurers of spring have already taken the plunge. The snowdrops were among the first on the scene, along with early crocuses. A few honey bees are buzzing around these earliest flowers. Catkins are appearing on the quaking aspens. Spring peepers are tuning up in the puddles left by retreating winter.

The "cheerily-chirrup" notes of the robins may be heard, along with a hopeful song sparrow every now and then. And one of the most reliable of all spring harbingers, the woodcock's aerial courtship flight, was heard last evening.

More cautious feelers are being put out by the daffodils, amaryllis, primroses, and hyacinths, as their leaves are beginning to show above the ground. Moreover, the observing eye may see other signs of adventuresomeness on the part of nature: The buds of the maples are beginning to redden, and those of forsythia, lilacs, dogwood, and peach trees look anxious to open. There is also a yellowish-green tinge appearing on the willow trees.

It does not take too much imagination and optimism to feel the rush that will soon begin to gladden the landscape. Relying on past records, some of the best-known flowers should be coming upon the scene between the end of March and the middle of April, roughly in the following order: forsythia, daffodils, hyacinths, primroses, magnolias, bloodroot, peach blossoms, violets (Edwin Way Teale, in his book entitled *North with the Spring,* called the violet the "emblem of the North American spring"[10]), forget-me-nots, cherry and pear blossoms, and spring beauties. With them will come the warblers, the house wrens and others to assure us that again we may begin to think of removing the storm windows.

Oh, yes, we should not let our joy run away with us. Ground hogs will soon be out again to help themselves in the garden; and onion grass and dandelions will be around to make the lawn keeper's life a busy one. And, by the way, you might as well start planning to cut the grass about the middle of April.

October 5 —
Snow flurries today —
Canada geese flying south two
days now — discussing as they go —
with winter
trailing behind.

What is it the Canada's stir in us?

Autumn trees beautiful — grey sky doesn't seem
to tone down these colors mixed in
heaven.

Carol Deckung

High on the list of nature's most mysterious and fascinating events must be bird migration, mysterious to professional ornithologists, who have yet to figure out just how birds find their way on their often very long and hazardous trips, and fascinating to the rest of us, just because it happens.

Early on a recent October morning, one of my favorite events of the fall took place: The white-throated sparrows were back with us again, tuning up in the underbrush on the way down toward our brook. I wondered just where they kept cool during the hot summer. Was it up in the Poconos or the Adirondacks? Or was it in New Hampshire or Maine? And just how on earth did they find their way back to our underbrush again, assuming (probably safely) that at least some of them were here with us last fall and winter?

Whatever the answers, the white throats are back again with us in Princeton, New Jersey, occasionally giving us snatches of their lovely, plaintive song, poorly translated as, "Old Sam Peabody, Peabody, Peabody . . ." or, by the more romantic, "Darling I love you, true, true, true. . . ." Still more frequently heard in the fall are their shorter notes, which sound as if they are "chinking together" whatever change they may have left in their pockets.

Numerous theories have been advanced to explain how birds find their way during migration, but none have really dispelled the mystery of it all. They do not appear to be guided solely by the physical characteristics of the land over which they fly, although some, such as hawks, do follow mountain ridges, which produce air currents to help them on their way. Studies, in various stages of inconclusiveness, suggest that birds may be guided by the position of the sun, the moon, the stars, the planets, or even by the earth's magnetic field.

Except when severe storms upset their movements, weather conditions seem to affect only slightly where they go and how fast they go. Just to complicate matters further, some species, such as blue jays and cardinals, migrate little if at all. The availability of food is, of course, a factor of prime importance in determining where they go.

A good deal of migration usually escapes our attention, since it takes place at night, although occasionally the listening ear may pick up faint voices overhead, and small forms may be seen crossing the face of the moon. Many birds are killed at night as they fly into lighthouses or other tall, lighted obstacles, such as the Washington Monument. Night migrants often spend the day down with us, stocking up on food for their next nightly flight.

Some migration, of course, takes place by day, as in the case of swallows, who feed on insects, and hawks. What we see during the day often deepens the mystery of it all. All of us have seen large clouds of grackles, red-winged blackbirds, and robins wheeling about overhead during the daylight hours, often not heading in the direction the season would indicate, perhaps getting their bearings.

One incident especially stands out in my memory. One clear October day I was watching a sizeable V-formation of Canada Geese heading southward, high overhead, honking as they went. Along came an airliner at about the same height as the geese, its direction intercepting theirs. Gradually and majestically, the V changed direction, made a complete circle, then resumed its southward flight through the recent path of the plane. Was it self-preservation that motivated the leaders of the V? Or could it have been curiosity to see what that queer and noisy contraption was, so recently added to obstruct their ancient right of way?

The Changing of the Guard

May 31 —

Blackpoll warbler in spruce tree — high, thin call, louder in middle — looks like a chickadee in striped pajamas. Canada warbler here too. Many beautiful warblers passing through all month. Winter friends quietly leaving — spring arrivals filling the places.

Carol Decker

As spring replaces winter in the Princeton area, the attention of almost everyone is caught by the delightful floral parade passing by. Generally less noticed are the changes that take place in our bird population.

The beautiful, haunting notes of the white-throated sparrow are soon to be heard no more in this area until the fall brings them back again from their northern summer resorts. Also to be missed from our bird feeders for the summer will be the red-breasted nuthatches and juncos.

Certain changes are hardly noticeable. For example, while some species are to be found here throughout the year, individuals of some of those species tend to migrate north and south with the seasons. That is, while robin *A,* who spent the winter with us, may move north with the coming of spring, robin *B,* who spent the winter somewhere south of us, may replace robin *A* in our locality for the summer.

In any event, certain birds may be seen here all year including crows, tufted titmice, chickadees, mourning doves, blue jays, mocking birds, along with several kinds of hawks, owls, and woodpeckers.

Probably the most noticeable of the changes in our bird population are of two major types: First, some of the most beautiful species use our part of the country largely as a refueling stop on their flyways to their northern nesting grounds, providing us with only a brief and tantalizing look at them. These include many of the warblers. If you have not seen and heard a magnolia warbler, a black-throated green warbler, or a

Blackburnian warbler, you have a special treat waiting for you early some May morning, provided you can get up that early.

The second change is that, fortunately, many species move up here from their winter habitats, which are often in Latin America, and stay with us to nest during the summer, thus giving us a good chance to get to know them. These include some of our most beautiful singers, such as the wood thrush, the Baltimore and orchard orioles, and the yellow warbler.

Among the many other summer residents in this area, the following are perhaps among the better known: house wren, catbird, scarlet tanager, yellow-breasted chat, kingbird, barn swallow, and red-eyed vireo.

And don't forget to be on the lookout for that gem of all gems—the ruby-throated hummingbird. The hummingbird may have flow 500 miles straight across the Gulf of Mexico in one night just so that you could see him.

July 1 —
Eastern phoebe singing
his name from
the wire leading
to the barn —

raspy
– phoebe
– phoebe
– phoebe

while his
mate sits
on second

♂

wags tail
down

nest inside
the door.

Carol Decker

The common names of birds—those usually used by birders and which are found in the bird guides—have been acquired in all sorts of ways.

We are not talking here about their Latin names, scientifically sorted out by professional ornithologists and rarely even noticed by the rest of us. Nor do we need to get into the confusion created by the numerous names used in different localities for the same species (for example, one of the books on my desk lists no less than eight other names for the red-tailed hawk).

Perhaps our favorite names for birds, since they are easiest to remember, are the ones the birds themselves call out to us. What could be more simple, direct, and memorable than the call of "chick-a-dee," even though a few more "dees" are often added and even though it might confuse us a bit at first by throwing in a "fee-bee" now and then? Thumbing through a bird guide soon gives us similar examples of birds that tell us who they are: "whip-poor-will," "bobwhite," "killdeer," "phoebe," and many others.

Attempts to translate into our inadequate language what birds say to us do not always come out the same way. For example, on a recent bird walk at the Stony Brook–Millstone Watersheds Association for some grade schoolers, I asked them to write down what they heard the birds say to them. On checking over their notes, I came upon one bird that had said "stink." Though a bit puzzled at first, I soon found that the recorder had thus heard the call "chewink."

The character of the notes of certain birds has also led to the names by which they are known. The call of the mourning dove seems to explore the depths of sorrow and sadness.

Many other reasons may be found for the names given to birds. For example, the physical appearance of the following birds no doubt led to their names: spoonbill, great horned owl, bluebird (though in this case, as in many others, its name is far from completely descriptive of the bird's appearance).

The names of the marsh hawk and the meadow lark were probably based on where they are most commonly found. The Nashville warbler is said to have been discovered first by Alexander Wilson at Nashville, Tennessee, and it has kept that name ever since.

The bird's behavior is often the basis for its name: brown creeper, black skimmer, woodpecker, ovenbird (whose nest is supposed to be shaped like an oven).

Occasionally, a person's name is included as part of a bird's common name, presumably to honor the part that person played in first identifying the bird; for example: Bell's vireo (said to be named by Audubon for a friend) and Kirtland's warbler.

Rarely, fortunately, is the name commonly given a bird not on target at all. Who ever heard a screech owl screech?

Just to complicate things a bit, professional ornithologists, for reasons often not clear to the rest of us, change the names of birds to new ones, which are supposed to be used from then on by those "in the know." For example, the former myrtle warbler is now supposed to be the yellow-rumped warbler, the towhee (or chewink) has become the rufous-sided towhee, the blue-headed vireo is now the solitary vireo.

All of this adds up to the fact that there is considerable inconsistency in the reasons birds receive the names by which they are commonly known. However, we may happily make our way through this maze as we remember Ralph Waldo Emerson's comment that "A foolish consistency is the hobgoblin of little minds."

Why Do
Birds Sing?

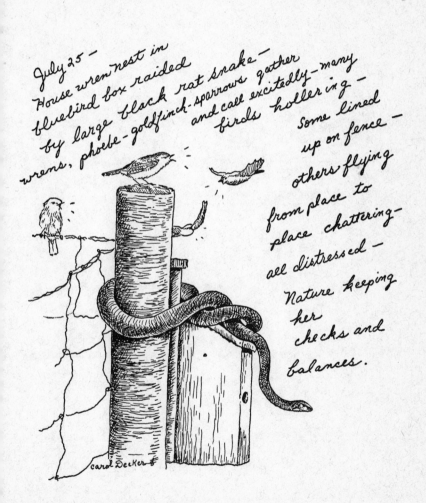

July 25 —
House wren nest in
bluebird box raided
by large black rat snake—
wrens, phoebe—goldfinch—sparrows gather
and call excitedly—many
birds hollering—
Some lined
up on fence—
others flying
from place to
place chattering—
all distressed—
Nature keeping
her
checks and
balances.

carol Decker

A recent program on public television was entitled "Why Do Birds Sing?" While the ideas advanced and the methods and equipment used to explore this matter were very interesting, the program did not fully answer—at least for me—the intriguing question posed by its title.

The answers given as to why birds sing (or call) seemed to fall under three major headings. First, birds sing in their nesting grounds in order to shoo away others from the vicinity of their nests. Striking evidence of this was given in the program, and it is easily duplicated by anyone who plays a tape or record of the notes of a certain species near where others of that same species are nesting. Their excited and menacing reaction is clearly evident as they fluff up their feathers and dive at the recorder. There is no question how they feel about the threat from the supposed intruder, and how much they want to get rid of it.

Second, the program gave examples of how birds utter alarm notes when they discover a predator such as a hawk or an owl in their vicinity. Such warnings appear also to serve as calls to others for help in mobbing the predator; and these calls are often heeded by birds of different species, so that the mob usually turns out to be a rather motley one.

The third reason given was that the males (who do most of the calling or singing) do so to attract mates. No matter that the program did not give any persuasive evidence on this point. Ever since the time of Adam it has been standard practice for males to whistle when they see a pretty girl go by.

But these reasons do not seem to explain why

birds sing under other circumstances. For example, on an early morning in May when the warblers and other migrants have stopped temporarily to feed on their way north, they fill the air with glorious music.

Why? They certainly are not protecting their nesting territory, for that is further along on their journey. No hawks or owls are to be seen nearby. They do not seem to be busy along the lines of attracting mates. I would hazard the guess that they are just commenting happily on the fun they are having feeding themselves on those luscious bugs.

Also, in the fall, groups of birds seem to sing and call to one another for no apparent reason except, perhaps, for the conviviality of the exercise. For example, a sizeable number of white-throated sparrows generally take up residence in a jungle of blackberry bushes down toward our brook when summer leaves. Any time of the day, but especially in the early morning, their beautiful plaintive notes may be heard, making the coming of winter seem less ominous. Are they just chatting, perhaps to assure one another that all will be well in spite of the cold days ahead?

Lewis Thomas, in *The Lives of a Cell,* comments on the singing of birds:

> Birdsong has been so much analyzed for its content of business communication that there seems little time left for music, but it is there. . . .
>
> The thrush in my backyard sings down his nose in meditative, liquid runs of melody, over and over again, and I have the strongest impression that he does this for his own pleasure. . . .
>
> It is a meditative, questioning kind of music, and I cannot believe that he is simply saying, "thrush here."[11]

Part Two

Getting to Know Some of the More Common Species of Birds

June 28 —
at the end of the
day a gathering of swallows
line up on the wire over the
lake appearing as spectators
to a great sport.

carol Decker

Are they perhaps
"Birdwatchers" watching
those that watch them?

The American Robin

April 2 —
Robin hunting
worms in the
yard — yanks,
tugs, pulls —

gotcha!

Carol Decker

Of all the birds, American robins are among the best known. This is partly because they are so numerous and widely distributed, but also because they seem to like the environment around our houses. Our structures apparently provide agreeable nesting spots for them; moreover, our lawns are good places to find earthworms, one of their favorite foods.

The robin's cheerful song is one of the first heard in the early morning and one of the last as day departs. While not as musical as some bird songs, his "cheerily-cheerup," often repeated over and over, is surely one of those best calculated to put one in a good humor, if we will but pause to listen to it. The robin also has a number of call and alarm notes, one sounding something like "chut-chut," as well as a variety of others of one or more syllables. One of the robin's notes not recognized by many bird listeners is a high sibilant hissing sound, usually delivered as he is sitting quietly in a tree.

Our "robin red breast" actually has a brown breast; his back is gray, and his head and tail are quite black. The bill is yellow. The young have conspicuous spots on their breasts, but these disappear as they grow up. It has been noted that these spots on the young identify the robin, though only temporarily, as being related to the thrush family.

The robin is a common sight on many lawns usually hopping but sometimes running in search of earthworms. When he feels success is near, he pauses, and often cocks his head to one side in an attitude of deep concentration. If satisfied, the robin plunges his bill into the ground and not infrequently comes up with one end of a worm. Then ensues a monumental tug of war, with the robin leaning back on his heels and behaving for all the world like a fisherman who has hooked into a big one.

How does he locate that worm when it is below the surface of the ground? Does he hear the worm? Does he see the earth move ever so slightly? One researcher on the subject has concluded that the robin locates the worm by sight rather than sound.[12]

It should be added that robins also feed on a number of insects as well as on fruit of various kinds. They certainly are fond of cherries and usually get to them just before we do.

The arrival of robins is sometimes considered a sure sign that spring has come. However, a few are found along the coast up into New England throughout the winter. Individual robins migrate north and south as the seasons change, so that those which nest farthest north may spend the winter in the Middle Atlantic states. They then are often found in flocks and are relatively quiet and shy. Their "cheerily-cheerup" note, more than their mere presence, is the true harbinger of spring as the days begin to lengthen and grow warm and as their nesting activities begin again.

When the young do come, the parents are kept very busy feeding them from dawn to dusk. Then it is that the robins, along with many other species, might very well ask who invented the expression "eating like a bird" and they might well challenge the usual meaning associated with that expression.

March 11 — Just caught male cardinal feeding female — Spring is here.
He courts his mate with food, the "proverbial box of candy."

She's just beautiful! a warm rosy sunrise seems to glow on her breast feathers on such a grey March day.

She looks like a young bird begging food from a parent.

The cardinal (also sometimes called redbird or cardinal grosbeak) makes himself known to almost all of us by his brilliant colors, cheerful songs, stately or even autocratic behavior, and because he does not seem to shun the presence of humans.

The striking attire of the male is probably the first thing to catch our attention. The name "cardinal" is related to his generally brilliant red color. The red is especially bright on his underparts, becoming tinged with grey on his back. Offset against this is his jet black forehead, sideburns, and beard. His bill is large (hence the occasional use of the name *grosbeak*) and reddish, and his general appearance is made still more noticeable by his active red crest. This he (or she) often raises, presumably to indicate emotions of fear, joy, or anger and lowers it again to give the "all-clear" signal. Mrs. Cardinal's garb is much more demure, the brilliant red of her mate generally being replaced by light brown, although she does sport his active crest, large reddish bill with its black surroundings, and some reddish tinges on her wings and tail.

The note of the cardinal is full of sunny cheerfulness. It is one of the first to be heard on an early spring morning. Although it is extremely varied, it still has a basic quality that allows it to be identified, with practice, as that of the cardinal. The female cardinal sings as well as the male. This is somewhat unusual among birds. Her note is very sweet and somewhat softer than his. Their call note is a soft "chip," with a good deal of music in it.

The male, especially, is often quite belligerent

around bird feeders, brooking little competition from others, especially other male cardinals. He will sometimes even pick a fight with his reflection in a window! On the other hand, he is often seen tenderly feeding his mate during courtship and while she is on the nest. He is also solicitous in helping to care for the young.

Cardinals move about some as the seasons change, but they do not migrate as much as most birds do and are generally with us all winter. Their nests are usually found in low bushes and give the appearance of having been rather hastily put together, though they are quite well concealed.

Cardinals may be coaxed near the house by scattering seeds on the ground and by putting up bird feeders. Their particular favorite seems to be sunflower seeds, although they will also go for the less-expensive seed mixtures. At the bird feeder, cardinals display the interesting habit of appearing to savor the seeds, rolling them thoughtfully around in their mouths, with their beaks kept partly open, before swallowing them.

The Blue Jay

July 10 — Bluejay sun-bathing in the yard. Jay raises one wing, exposes underside and breast feathers to sun's rays for warmth. Feathers are fluffed out — tail fanned ↓

cocks head to side ↓

carol Decker

Just occurred to me — I'm enjoying the sun too.... while I watch. Don't we go to the beach?

As fall arrives, most birds tend to quiet down in color as well as in conversation, but not the blue jay. His (as well as her) striking blue, black, and white plumage then seems even more brilliant against the colors of the foliage than at other times of the year; and, for some reason, while the majority of birds tend to be seen more than heard during the fall, the blue jay (frequently in competition with the crow) loudly tells us of his presence. His active crest adds to his "cock-of-the-walk" behavior.

Everything considered, the blue jay is about the most conspicuous bird of the fall season. His usual call is a harsh, often repeated rendition of his name: "jay! jay! jay!" Yet the blue jay often surprises the listener with other notes, including a not unmusical, clear, bell-like note that he utters more generally in the spring than in the fall.

The blue jay's behavior matches his loud colors and noisy calls. He is one of the leading "bad guys" of the bird world and is a center of controversy wherever he is found. Apparently the blue jay earns the love of none of his neighbors.

Blue jays have often been caught in the act of robbing the nests of smaller birds and ruthlessly killing their young. In recognition of this, one of the names by which he is known is "nest robber."

However, not only does the blue jay pick on smaller and defenseless prey, but he does not hesitate to make life miserable for the most redoubtable of his enemies—the great horned owl. In fact, one of the best ways to locate an owl in the woods in the daytime is to go where a crowd of blue jays, often accompanied by crows and robins, are badgering the owl, making a terrific din as they tell him loudly and exactly just what they think of him.

Clearly we have in the blue jay a colorful as well as a questionable character. James Whitcomb Riley captured an important part of the blue jay's personality when he wrote in his poem "Knee Deep in June":

> Mr. blue jay, full o'sass,
> In them base-ball clothes of his,
> Sportin' round the orchard jes'
> Like he owned the premises.[13]

July 13 — Watching a catbird this
morning eating wild blackberries
in yard. He balances on
moving branch with tail
fanned in and out →

Catbird
perches against a sky
tinted pink and sings most
evenings — much to my pleasure.
I'll share the blackberries with
him in the mornings.

Carol Decker

Of all the birds out in the countryside during the month of June, the catbird stands out as an especially distinct and intriguing personality. He (or she) is obviously very much interested in what you are doing in the garden, whatever you are doing.

His curiosity exhibits itself not only in his keeping an eye on you, but also in his comments along the way. Though they come steadily and persistently, these comments are not an irritating intrusion on that privacy and quiet which many gardeners cherish, for you may listen or not, take them or leave them.

They merely provide an interesting background for your communing with nature, one of the chief rewards of gardening.

There's no question about it, however, he (it is usually the male) is talkative. What's more, he uses a great number of sounds to express whatever he has on his mind. Included is a catlike "mew" (hence his name), along with a great variety of sweet melodies and harsh and squeaky discords.

Among the curiosities found in the bird books is the statement, in three of the five on my desk, to the effect that the catbird rarely repeats the phrases he uses. Can the authors really have listened to a catbird in full swing? Certainly not our catbird.

He not only often repeats certain phrases that apparently appeal to him, but he also frequently experiments with various new endings to these phrases before he moves on to new ones. As a matter of fact, you never can tell what to expect from him next. The results are most comical and entertaining.

The bird books also disagree about whether or not he is a good imitator of other birds' songs: One book says he is; another says he is a poor imitator; two say he is "somewhat of a mimic." What is one to believe? The answer would seem to be that you can read almost anything you want into what you hear from him. In any event, he seems to have plenty of original ideas of his own, not needing to copy those of anyone else.

While the male's notes and songs are loud, his garb is not. His basic attire is a quiet gray, and his cap is black. The feathers under his tail (which he often jerks to emphasize his words) are chestnut in color.

Our garden companion is not without his critics. Some say he robs the nests of other birds; in fact, John Burroughs, as noted in *Birds of America,* stated that he had seen a catbird do this.[14] If so, perhaps the catbird belongs under surveillance for such acts of atrocity, along with many of our own species.

No doubt about the fact that the catbird makes off with many things to which he has no legal right, including berries and fruits of various sorts. But, along with these, one study showed that 44 percent of the catbird's diet is made up of ants, beetles, caterpillars, grasshoppers, and spiders, things few of us value as garden companions.

Everything considered, here's one vote for allowing the catbird to stay on the loose as an effective insecticide, as well as to provide us with pleasurable conversation and company in the garden.

The Chickadee

Little aerial acrobat —
always hanging
from something
upside down.

March 2 —
Went out to fill
bird feeder. Impatient
chickadee scolding me
"to hurry up."
Decided instead to coax him
to my hand for sunflower seeds. Only
took 5 minutes. He came to my hand
twice — I could hardly feel
this tiny bit of fluff land. Did he just
enter my world or I his?

There is nothing that gladdens a winter's day like a blackcapped chickadee. The more bitter the wind, the deeper the snow, and the darker the day, the more his (or her) youthful exuberance seems to bubble forth to soften the scene.

He appears to have the acrobatics of youth built into his makeup. He weighs only about an ounce, but he certainly has bounce in that ounce. He seems just as happy exploring the world upside down as right side up. Rarely does he sit still for long. There is too much of interest going on for that. He interviews every passerby and pries into every nook and cranny. Someone has called him a feathered question mark.

His curiosity, however, is not offensive, for he nearly always appears good-humored as he searches his surroundings. He generally retreats gracefully from the scene when he is seriously challenged, although occasionally he does not hide his displeasure at being displaced from a choice spot at the bird feeder.

His willingness to make friends with humans is outstanding. The chickadee is one of the most enthusiastic about what he is offered at the bird feeder. Furthermore, he is probably the first to be willing to eat trustfully out of the hands of those who are patient enough. It seems to help if we talk softly to him about the world's problems as we hold out the seeds (preferably sunflower) to him and if we are able to stifle that sneeze at the critical moment.

Members of the chickadee family are with us all year long, so that it should not be hard to get to know them. The blackcap is said to move north and south with the seasons, but there are some individuals of the species with us at all times.

To clinch the matter of identification, the black cap comes about as close as any bird to telling us his name with his "chick-a-dee-dee-dee." He also has a plaintive two-call note sounding something like "fee-bee" (the first syllable is a note or two higher than the second). This becomes a four-syllable "fee-bee, fee-bee" in the case of his otherwise very similar Southern cousin, the Carolina chickadee, also found in New Jersey.

His garb (the sexes are similar in coloration) is an exquisite combination of black, white, and gray, which he always keeps neat as a pin. His black cap and black bib are set off to perfection against the white sides of his head. His sides are generally washed lightly with brown.

His diet consists largely of things we would just as soon do without: spiders, tent caterpillars (and their moths and eggs), along with many other destructive insects. When he turns to fruit and berries, these are usually the kind not especially useful to humans.

All of this adds up to the fact that in the chickadee we have a perky, trustful, useful, and generally attractive friend—a good friend to have around.

The Flicker

June 27—

Flickers nesting in tree outside window— Can watch at eye level. Parents feed young by regurgitating food. Both youngsters have male's black moustache. Last night light from room disturbed young flickers and they buzzed loudly for several minutes until the light went out.

Red patch

♀
no black moustache on cheek

Carol Decker

The flicker seems to have discovered one of the secrets of success for getting along in this world: Be conspicuous.

His garb alone would make him the center of attention in any teen-age bird gang. The yellow-shafted flicker (the one found in the Princeton area) wears a small red scarf on the back of his neck, a black scarf at his throat, and black beads all over his chest.

When he flies, bright yellow is displayed under his wings and white flashes from his rump. Also, just to make sure he is "with it," the male sports a black mustache!

The flicker comes fairly close to pronouncing his name with his rather soft "flicka, flicka, flicka." At other times, he really makes the welkin ring with something like a rapid "flick, flick, flick" or a clear, descending "kleeah."

His behavior is also distinctive. He hops (does not walk) around the yard looking for food (mostly ants) in stiff, general-of-the-army fashion. When he flies, he generally roller-coasters his way toward his destination, very much like a gold finch.

However, his occasional early morning capers, especially in the spring, really set him apart. Think you would like to catch that last extra bit of sleep before the alarm clock goes off, do you? The flicker frequently has other ideas. He puts the alarm clock to shame by drumming with his beak on any available noisy part of the house, such as a tin roof or a drain pipe. And what a racket he can make!

You may wave him off or slow him down by

shouting at him, but he appears to get such puckish enjoyment from the scene that he often returns to his fun, just as you attempt to settle down again.

One of my friends thought he had this problem licked a few years back. It was spring, and daylight-saving time was about to arrive. So, of course, the flicker would be an hour late the next morning. Fine, or so my friend thought. But it did not work that way. The flicker merely arrived an hour earlier with the advent of the new time schedule.

Or so my friend claimed—and you can almost count on his veracity.

March 14 — Watching a crow break similar sized twigs from a dead part of our white pine tree. Made repeated trips to nest site in woods and back for more twigs.

carol Decker

crows are paired, whispering together at the tops of trees — the beginning of "new crows".

The crow has become such a part of our environment that he has even taken over some of the ways in which we express ourselves. For instance, if we want to go by the most direct route from one place to another, we go "as the crow flies." If we undergo particularly distasteful humiliation for some misdeed, we "eat crow."

Our literature abounds with mentions of the crow. The power of Shakespeare is frequently enhanced by his references to the world of nature, among which are a number of cases where a crow comes on the stage. For example, in *Romeo and Juliet,* Benvolio, in trying to persuade Romeo that he may find others fairer than Rosaline (with whom Romeo is enamored up to that point in the play), promises, "Compare her face with some that I shall show, and I will make thee think thy swan a crow."[15] Juliet, soon thereafter, fulfills Benvolio's promise. And in *Macbeth,* after Duncan's foul murder, and after Macbeth has just planned Banquo's murder, the scene is further darkened when Macbeth comments:

> Come, seeling night,
> Scarf up the tender eye of pitiful day,
> ....
> .....Light thickens, and the crow
> Makes wing to the rooky wood.[16]

There is little doubt that most people recognize a crow when they see one. For one thing, they are quite common and are with us throughout the year, although they do migrate to some extent. The complete inky blackness of the crow's plumage, from tip to toe, is quite familiar to all. His usual "caw, caw, caw" is frequently heard. (He has two cousins, both also inky black: the fish crow, slightly smaller and found more in the South, with a shorter and less emphatic "car" or "chu-hu" call; and the northern raven, slightly larger and found more in northern climes, with more of a roll to his "k-r-ruk.").

The crow's behavior is less well-known in all its variableness, and it is worthy of comment, partly because there is so much of interest about it, as well as so many superstitions surrounding it.

The crow's diet includes just about anything edible, animal or vegetable. They have an especially great appetite for newly sprouted corn and love to make off with it just as it comes up through the ground. Most farmers would generally agree, especially those that raise corn, that all crows should be shot on sight!

Crows do not seem to get along well with other species of birds. They are known to feed on the eggs and young of other birds, who are often seen attempting to chase them away from their nests. Also, they are frequently seen and heard in mobs, often in the company of blue jays and robins, making life unpleasant for hawks and owls. In a popularity contest, they would generally not fare well at all.

To match their general unpopularity, they apparently have learned to be wary. There is quite good evidence that, when they are conducting their depredations, they post sentries to warn the others of any impending danger. The sentry gives a particularly sharp alarm call to a flock of crows feeding in a corn-field, for example, when he sees a farmer approaching with a gun. How much else they are able to communicate to one another, perhaps through a special crow language, is a matter of considerable debate and some superstition.

One point does, however, stand out about the crow and his language. This point may be introduced by quoting Shakespeare again. In *The Merchant of Venice,* Portia remarks to Nerissa: "The crow does sing as sweetly as the lark, when neither is attended."[17] Edwin Way Teale gave us a partial confirmation of Shakespeare's astonishing knowledge on this matter when he wrote in *A Naturalist Buys an Old Farm:*

> Anyone who fancies that crows utter only a "caw" should have been in my brush pile on those June days when a family of these birds alighted among the brook-side trees. Sitting silent and unseen—I became absorbed in noting the variations in volume, in inflection, in tone, in tempo, in emphasis—in a word in how wide a vocabulary they employed.[18]

Others have reported hearing crows warble softly. But most are skeptical of tales about their holding trials and condemning and killing those of their number whom they have found "guilty" of some offense.

A final comment about the behavior of this re-markable bird: Observations made of crows, both wild as well as tamed, indicate that they are very clever, and that they have pronounced tendencies toward kleptomania. Apparently they have a strong desire to steal and hide all sorts of objects, especially those that are shiny or brightly colored.

Thus, the crow should get very high marks for his interesting character, even if not for his general popularity.

May 10 —
Yesterday I
brushed the dog in
the yard — this morning the
wren is recycling the dog's
hair into its nest. Back
again for more hair to line
the twig nest in the wren house.

One year wren tried
to nest in jeans pocket
drying on the line.
Last year it chose
the open mailbox. We put
out a new wren house
over the mailbox & "Jenny"
moved in —
The mailman thanked
me!

Carol Decker

It may come as a surprise to some of the many fans of Jenny (as well as Johnny) Wren that their behavior has been the subject of considerable controversy over the years. These energetic little mites, generally thought of as bubbling over with innocent merriment, have all too frequently been caught in the act of destroying the eggs, nests, and young of other birds living in their vicinity. In 1925, one Miss Sherman even wrote an article entitled "Down with the House Wren Boxes."[19] Defenders of the wrens, on the other hand, have noted that they are merely engaging in the struggle for survival going on throughout the world of nature. What a price to pay for "free enterprise" in the competition for food and places to live!

Whichever side you may take in this controversy, the house wren surely engages one's attention. This is not because the male or female, which look very much alike, are eye catching in size or color. They are only about five inches long, smaller than most sparrows. They are also quite undistinguished in color, being generally brownish above, barred with some black, and somewhat lighter underneath. The observing eye is caught, however, by the action of the perky tail, which gives a good indication of the wren's disposition.

When it comes to the sounds the house wren makes, however, one is soon convinced that here is other than a run-of-the-mill character. Shaking all over with apparent excitement as he announces his presence to the world, the house wren is extremely talkative and gives every indication of being very sure of himself. His song bubbles explosively upward in a burst of enthusiasm and falls in tone at the end, the individual notes tumbling all over one another. When one approaches too close to his nest or young, his harsh, grating chatter would put to shame the scolding of Dame Van Winkle. All in all, although the wren's song has a merry quality to it, he is remarkably noisy for so small a bird and can almost become irritating as he repeats it over and over again. The behavior of the house wren fits in with his song. He is extremely energetic and seems irritable, nervous, and jumpy.

Wrens' nesting habits are especially interesting and eccentric. They build their nests almost anywhere and with almost any materials available. Although they are eager occupants of bird boxes, their nests may just as often be found in the most amazing places, such as old tin cans, holes in trees, buildings, machinery, nests of other birds, drain pipes, and even in pockets of old clothes left hanging in available places! However variable their choice of nesting places may be, there is good evidence that the parent birds return to the same spot year after year.

The materials used in building the nests are almost as diversified. Small sticks or weed stems seem to be the favorites, but nails and other pieces of metal are sometimes used. Whatever the materials may be, they usually are stuffed into the nests in such amounts that the entrance is almost blocked to possible intruders, as well as to the parents themselves.

And, speaking of keeping intruders out, one of the useful things to remember in building a wren house is to make the entry hole no larger than a twenty-five-cent piece. This will make it reasonably sure that Eng-

lish sparrows, starlings, and cowbirds will not be able
to get in.

Jenny and Johnny Wren certainly are distinctive
personalities. Whatever depredations they may inflict
on their neighbors and however noisy they may be,
their arrival from the south is a sure sign that spring
has come.

The Slate-Colored Junco

January 24 — Juncos and other winter seed eaters flying or hopping up to catch seed heads. shake & let go. Seeds spill out on snow & all birds feed on them — cooperating ! to survive the winter.

chickadees & tree sparrows also seen riding on stems — dislodging seeds.

Black-eyed pusan

Carol Decker

Whether or not you like cold weather, there is one thing that may make a cold winter's day considerably more attractive. Find a cozy spot to watch your bird feeder some day after the snow is newly fallen. There is a certain amount of bustle and confusion in the air. Titmice and chickadees vie for preferred spots at the feeder, with the titmice almost always having their way. A white-breasted nuthatch or two may join the others and perhaps a downy woodpecker, especially if there is suet to be had. A blue jay arrives, contributing to the color of the scene, and even more brilliance may be added by a male cardinal.

One of the chief actors in this scene is very often the gentle and unobtrusive junco, appropriately known as the "snowbird" by many people. He is usually to be seen feeding on the ground under the feeder, frequently in the company of a white-throated sparrow, which also seems to prefer ground feeding. These two appear to be perfectly content to accept the seeds that have been dislodged from the feeder and discarded from above by the more choosy titmice and chickadees.

The name "snowbird" goes well with the migrating habits and behavior of the junco. He is with us all winter throughout most of the Eastern states, cavorting about in the snowiest and coldest weather. His flashing white outer tail feathers are pure snow in color. He is often seen in flocks along roadsides in the winter, as well as at bird feeders. With the departure of winter, he leaves the low lands of New Jersey—usually in late April—and goes further north or to higher elevations to spend the summer breeding season.

Juncos are related to sparrows, which they resemble in shape and size, being 5½ to 6½ inches long. They are generally dark above and white below, thus appearing to be wearing their tuxedos upside down. Their bills are a light pink in color. Their white outer tail feathers, which flash as they fly about, are perhaps the best mark of all by which to distinguish them. The females and young are duller in color than the males, but all of them sport those white outer tail feathers.

Juncos are rather quiet while they are with us in the winter, when their calls are usually limited to what sounds like a short "tsack." In their breeding grounds in the summer, one hears their longer song, a chipping trill, somewhat like that of a chipping sparrow, but sweeter and with more music in it.

While the coming of spring brings more colorful birds to us, one hates to give up, in return, the presence of the cheery junco. We may, however, look forward to his return with the fall, when our more glamorous but less hardy summer residents depart for the south.

The
Tufted
Titmouse

January 15 —
Beautiful melon sunrise but - 5°F
bitter cold & windy. Birds
only move to come to feeder —
saving on all possible
energy.

Tufted titmouse
conserving body heat
by fluffing out feathers →

occasionally can
see little puffs of
bird breath on frosty air
as birds feed.

wind
blows tail
back &
forth

Carol Decker

The clear ringing notes of the tufted titmouse may be heard pretty much throughout the year in the Eastern states. He behaves and sounds as if he is enjoying himself, and his enthusiasm surely can add to our enjoyment, particularly on a cold early spring morning.

His usual longer note is of two syllables, repeated several times. Some say it sounds like "Peter-Peter-Peter." Our tufted titmouse, however, sounds more to us as if he were saying "chewy-chewy-chewy." This note may be repeated over and over again, especially if two of them are calling to each other from some distance apart, as they often seem to be doing. In fact, the one deeper in the woods often sounds like an echo, so closely do they imitate each other. He also frequently utters a clear single-syllable note.

The songs of a number of birds have a somewhat similar loud ringing quality about them, which sometimes makes it difficult for the beginner to tell them apart. For example, distinguishing between the notes of the titmouse, the cardinal, and the Carolina wren appears to be hard for some people. The problem seems to be made even more complicated by the fact that the same species may accent different syllables of its note in different localities. One of the ways to overcome this difficulty is to listen to the records of bird songs which have been made by organizations such as the Laboratory of Ornithology of Cornell University, and the National Geographic Society, among others. Such records are generally available at public libraries.

The titmouse also has a shorter and less friendly call note, a buzzy nasal "chay," sounding somewhat like a subdued "jay" of the blue jay.

Titmice are about 6 inches long—the size of a

large sparrow—but of more slender proportions than most sparrows. Their upper parts are a quiet gray while their underparts are white, except for their sides, which are brownish. Look for two other things in order to identify them: black beady eyes, which stand out clearly against their white cheeks; and a gray crest, which may or may not be raised, depending on the circumstances and their mood. Also, if you look very closely you will see that their foreheads are black. The sexes are similar in color.

The titmouse is an enthusiastic and gregarious customer at the bird feeder, seeming to enjoy the company especially of the chickadees. Maybe this is because he lords it over the chickadees, who seem to accept, without too much fuss, a lower position in the "pecking order." The titmouse also seems to accept human company and is said to be easy to tame. He does not seem to migrate to any great extent, though his range has extended further north in recent years, perhaps because of the increase in the number of feeders and his obvious liking for them.

One thing you will often see him do at the bird feeder (a habit shared to some extent by the chickadees): He carries a sizeable seed in his bill away from the feeder to a nearby limb, holds the seed with his feet, while he bangs it energetically with his bill until he opens it. He never seems to miss and hit his foot or to suffer from headaches.

May 23 —
Dandelions every-
where, so too are
the happy & cheerful
"wild canaries" —

Black
cap on
male's
head →

♂

Splashes of
hovering yellows
over the plants
that have
gone to
seed.
Enjoying goldfinches
several days
now.

Carol Decker

Take a flash of golden sunshine, offset against a black-and-white background, sprinkle liberally with music of the merriest sort imaginable, and you have the male goldfinch in the spring and summer. The gold covers all except his cap, which is black, and his wings and tail, which are a mixture of black and white. The female's garb is much more subdued, for she lacks the black cap and the bright golden body. In the winter he is colored much like his mate. Their bills, being short and conical, are clearly built for seed eating, although they do feed partly on insects in the summer. Goldfinches are about 5 inches in length, somewhat smaller than most sparrows.

They are known in some places as "wild canaries." They may be easily distinguished from other birds by their notes and calls. Perhaps the most noticeable call is the one they make with their roller-coaster flight. It sounds something like "Per-chick-oree" or "Just look at me," and it is generally delivered starting about at the bottom of one of the swings in his roller-coaster flight and ending roughly at the top of that swing, almost as if he were lifting himself toward heaven with his song. To further gladden his surroundings, he often lands near the top of a tree and pours forth a long canary-like statement about how the world is really a very good place in which to live. He also has a short and sweet call note, sounding like "zwee–zee," rising in tone at the end. While some of the loveliest bird songs are thoughtful and even sad, like those of the hermit thrush and the white-throated sparrow, the goldfinch is L'Allegro himself.

It is hard to know just what to say about the migratory behavior of the goldfinch. Certainly he is more in evidence in the spring and summer in New Jersey, partly because at these times the male dons his brightest colors and he is singing more. But he does migrate some. He is, however, frequently seen here during the winter, often at bird feeders.

The nesting habits of goldfinches are rather unusual, in that they nest somewhat later than other birds. This may be because they depend so much on thistledown in the construction of their nests, and thistles do not mature until July or August, well after most other birds have had at least their first brood of the season.

The Downy and Hairy Woodpeckers

January 1 – Noticed Downy woodpecker drinking sap on maple tree.

Warm winter days – very cold nights and sap running on all trees. Also noticed other songbirds drinking sap – another source of nourishment.

Red patch ↓

Except for one major difference, the downy and hairy woodpeckers could almost pass for twins. The difference is in their size: the downy is 6 to 7 inches in length (slightly larger than most sparrows), whereas the hairy is usually 9 to 10 inches long (just slightly smaller than a robin).

It is astonishing how nearly alike they are in all other respects. For example, both are found almost all over the United States, their ranges extending even up into Alaska, and they are likely to be found all over this area throughout the year. When it comes to their looks (other than their size), the experts usually point out only two ways in which these near twins differ, and most casual observers would probably not even notice such differences at all.

The first of these rather minor differences is that the downy has small black spots on his outer tail feathers, whereas these feathers are pure white on the hairy. Somewhat more noticeable is the fact that the bill of the hairy is a good deal larger than one would expect, when compared with that of the downy.

In all other respects, it is practically impossible to tell them apart by their coloration. The backs of both are a similar mixture of black and white, and their underparts are white. The males of both species have red patches on the backs of their heads, not found on the females. Both sexes of both species have black caps, white lines over their eyes, black patches through the eyes, and white cheeks. One of the important distinguishing features of both species, male and female, is the broad white stripe running down the middle of their backs. They are our only woodpeckers having such white backs and are sometimes called *white-backed woodpeckers*.

The notes of both species have a similar quality about them, but the hairy, as one might expect from his greater size, speaks with greater authority. His kingfisher-like drawn-out rattle is deeper and stronger than the high-pitched whinny of the downy; and the hairy's call note "penk" is louder than the downy's "tchick." Both may often be located before they are seen by the drumming noise they make as they drill into tree trunks in search of insects.

Again, one would hardly be able to tell downies from hairies by their behavior. They both are most industrious as they clamber about the trees, prying into crevices and under the bark, hunting for their favorite food—insects. They use their tails to help them inch higher, go sideways, or, on occasion, back down a bit. After having exhausted the prospects on one tree, they generally glide down to the bottom of another to start the search all over again. On longer trips their flight is undulating, somewhat like that of a goldfinch.

The downy is especially found around bird feeders. He appears most fond of suet, though he does take an occasional half-hearted try at the seeds. We have yet to see a hairy at our feeder, but we are hoping, since others report seeing them at theirs. There seem to be fewer hairies around, and they seem to be more shy, preferring the deep woods. Downies are quite gregarious, often coming to our feeders in company with waves of chickadees, titmice, nuthatches, and juncos. This, to turn the usual saying around, seems to indicate that birds not of a feather often flock together.

The fact that the hairy and downy woodpeckers are so nearly alike in almost all respects other than size may well be listed among the curiosities of a curious bird world.

November 19 —

White-breasted nuthatch

swaying back and forth with wings out,
tail fanned trying to scare other birds
that come too close at feeding station.
After a second or two of this, his bluff
usually doesn't work— he goes about
his business.

In his book, *An Introduction to Birds,* John Kieran tells about how, in his beginning birding days, he first learned about nuthatches.[20] In his capacity as teacher for a class of farm children, he was presented with a picture of a white-breasted nuthatch, which he was to use in teaching his class about that bird. It was pictured on a fence post and seemed to be perched upside down. So he turned the picture the other way around, only to find that the writing on the picture was then upside down. He finally concluded that the bird had been pictured upside down on purpose.

While they are most unusual among birds in this respect, nuthatches appear just as happy, or even more so, climbing down trees and posts head first as they search in the crevices and under the bark for their favorite insects.

There are three kinds of nuthatches found in the Eastern United States: the white-breasted, the red-breasted, and the brown-headed, and they are all "upside down" climbers. They all have short legs and strong toes tipped with sharp claws, which provide secure footing during their climbing acrobatics. In contrast to other climbers, such as woodpeckers, which usually climb upward using their long tails as props as they do so, the tails of the nuthatches are too short and stubby for such use.

The white-breasted nuthatch, the most common of the three, is found all over the East at any time of the year, moving little, if at all, with the seasons. He is especially fond of deciduous trees and is commonly found at bird feeders. He seems to be quite tame and gregarious and is often found in the company of chickadees, titmice, downy woodpeckers, juncos, and others.

The red-breasted nuthatch is somewhat more rare and seems a bit more choosy about the company he keeps, quite often being found with one or two others of his own species. He seems to prefer conifers and will occasionally come to bird feeders. He tends to be more northern in distribution and nesting habits, as a rule being found in New Jersey and further South only in the winter.

The brown-headed nuthatch is more Southern in distribution, usually found mainly below the Mason-Dixon Line. Like the red-breast, he displays a definite preference for conifers. Unlike the other two nuthatches, he usually occurs with others of his species in fair-sized flocks.

The three nuthatches are quite similar in build, with their stubby tails barely extending beyond their wing tips. Apart from that, they are quite easy to tell apart by their looks.

The white-breasted nuthatch is clearly larger than the other two nuthatches, being 5 to 6 inches long, about sparrow size. He has a bluish back with black and white wings, and the male has a black cap and nape. His beady black eyes stand out clearly against his white cheeks. His breast is white, with some brown on the flanks and under the tail.

The red-breasted nuthatch is about 4½ inches long. He also has a bluish back and a black cap. His distinguishing marks are a white line over the eyes and a black line through the eyes. Also, to live up to his name, his underparts are reddish brown.

The brown-headed nuthatch has a bluish back and white underparts, but a brown cap comes down just to the level of the eyes. Another distinguishing mark is a white spot on the back, just in back of the brown cap. Like the red-breast, he is about 4½ inches long.

The notes of the three are rather easy to tell apart. The call note of the white-breast sounds something like "yank-yank," and has a nasal quality about it. Sometimes this note is repeated rapidly and loudly, all on about the same key.

The red-breast is a good deal quieter. His call note has a nasal quality somewhat like that of the white-breasted nuthatch, but on a higher key. He also has a short high-pitched call sounding like "hit" or "hut."

The brown-headed nuthatch is a talkative midget with a high-pitched "pit–pit–pit," and a soft reedy, twittering note, quite different from the other two nuthatches.

One may be excused for wondering how on earth these three acquired the name of "nuthatch." Apparently, many years ago it was noticed in England that they had the habit of wedging nuts into crevices, and then hacking them open with their sturdy bills. The names "nuthack" and "nuthatch" were, it seems, used pretty much interchangeably, with "nuthatch" finally winning out. One can rest assured that their name has nothing to do with the hatching process.

The Brown-Headed Cowbird

April 7 — A pair of cowbirds courting. Male displaying and chasing female on ground. He dips or bows his head and arches his back —

Feathers fluffed out. Wings drop slightly as he walks around female while making his note. ↓

Carol Decker

♀

♂

I do not remember harboring many destructive tendencies in my youth, but I surely did develop one strong one: the desire to shoot every cowbird which came my way. As a result, quite a few of them had pretty narrow escapes after I acquired my "twenty-two" and the permission to use it.

This murderous leaning on my part, paradoxical as it may appear at first, was based on my love for birds, because, for every cowbird one sees, all or at least part of a nestful of young warblers, vireos, sparrows, or other small birds will very likely have perished. The reason for this is that the cowbird does not build her own nest or rear her own young. Rather, the female stealthily waits near the nest of one of her victims until the parent has left, then sneaks in to deposit an egg of her own in that nest. The owner of the nest may figure out what has happened and take counter measures, but very often she does not. If not, she incubates the cowbird's egg along with her own. Then, the young cowbird, once hatched, usually grabs most of the food brought to the nest by the parents (since young cowbirds are generally larger than the others) so that at least some of their young may starve. Later, one is likely to see the horrible sight of one young cowbird following its smaller foster parent around, begging noisily for food, which it almost invariably gets, so strong is the parental instinct.

Cowbirds perpetrate this parasitic act on a large number of different species. Some, like robins and catbirds, may get wise to what is going on and get rid of the cowbird's eggs. Others, like the yellow warbler, may realize that all is not right and build another nest layer above the original one where the cowbird has laid her egg. However, the cowbird often sneaks in again to lay another egg on the second nest layer, as well as on several higher layers if they are built. None of this endeared the cowbird to me as a young bird lover.

Cowbirds are about 6½ inches long, somewhat larger than house sparrows. They are often seen walking on the ground in yards or fields in the company of starlings, red-winged blackbirds, and grackles. The name "cowbird" is probably related to the fact that they quite often are seen near cattle, presumably waiting to feed on the insects stirred up as the cattle move about. They generally spend the winter in the Southern states, moving North in the summer.

The male cowbird is an iridescent black, except for his head, which is brown. The female is a very undistinguished mousy gray all over.

The sounds made by the cowbird are not pleasing to the ear. The male, as he shows off for his lady during the mating season, sounds a bit like a squeaky gate, meanwhile spreading his wings and tail as if in considerable pain or suffering from an upset stomach. He also whistles a high alarm note of several syllables, and gives a "chuck" something like that of a red-winged blackbird.

Many are the mysteries one encounters in the observation and study of birds. One of the strangest of these is why certain ones, like cowbirds (along with Old-World cuckoos and a number of other species) display such an unusual and very great indifference to incubating and caring for their young. Most animals (including humans, of course) show intense devotion to their offspring and are willing to take great risks to defend them. Not the indifferent cowbird!

June 11—
Spotted the red-
eyed vireo while I
was hanging laundry outside.
I'm probably the only lady who
hangs wash wearing binoculars!
Red-eye among maples
feeding and singing —
↙ probably nesting
nearby.

when I
see him
it's usually
here near brook and
woods — by the clothes
line, he sees me
in the same
place!

The red-eyed, warbling, white-eyed, solitary, and yellow throated vireos are alike in a number of ways. They are all about the same size or slightly smaller than a house sparrow. The sexes are similar in coloration. They all come back to us for the spring and summer, staying pretty much in our general area until they migrate South again to their winter quarters in the fall. The solitary and yellow-throated vireos seem to prefer to nest in the deeper woods and at higher altitudes than the others, for example, in the Poconos rather than in Princeton.

It is usually quite hard to get a good look at any of these five vireos, unless one happens to find a nest. This is because the yellow-throated vireo is an expert at performing a disappearing act in the low bushes, where he usually is found, while the other four spend most of their time high up in the trees. Looking for them up there soon becomes hard on the back of the neck, especially the older neck. (Unless a neck brace of some sort is devised, there are two possible solutions to this problem: Find a tree on which to lean the back of the head, so that the strain on the neck is relieved, or lie flat on the ground while looking up.)

The five can quite readily be told apart, however, by their looks (provided, of course, you can see them), and even more easily by their songs, which are very different from one another.

All but the yellow-throated vireo are rather inconspicuous in color. He has a bright yellow throat and breast and yellow "spectacles." His underparts are white. His back is grayish-green, and he has two white wing bars.

The white-eyed and solitary vireos also have grayish-green backs and white wing bars. Both have a light yellow wash on their sides and white underparts. The white-eyed vireo also has yellow "spectacles," whereas the solitary vireo has white ones. The solitary has a bluish head (he was formerly called the *blue-headed vireo*).

The red-eyed and warbling vireos lack wing bars and have grayish backs and lighter underparts. Both of them have white stripes over their eyes: that of the red-eyed vireo standing out clearly against the black-edged, blue-gray crown and that of the warbling vireo being less distinct.

Although it may be hard to see them clearly enough to tell them apart by their looks, their songs are something else again. Each vireo tells his own very different story when he takes over the sound waves.

The red-eyed is one of the most indefatigable talkers in the bird world. From morn to night, in the middle of the day, and on the hottest days, he often keeps right at it, with only short interruptions. For this reason, perhaps, he has been called the "preacher" or, by others more favorable to the clergy, the "senator." His phrases are short, sound a bit like broken-up bits of a robin's song, and are quite monotonous. His call note is a harsh "chay" or "pay."

The warbling vireo is more pleasant to listen to. He has a continuing warbling song that goes merrily up and down in tone for quite a while before he pauses for breath. This song is charming and unmistakable once you get to know it. Like the red-eyed vireo, he may sing away in the middle of the hottest day.

The song of the solitary vireo is composed of relatively short couplets or triplets, often slurred together and with longer pauses between them than in the red-eyed vireo's note. One word that best describes his note is "sweet." The effect is very pleasing.

The timing of the notes and phrases of the yellow-throated vireo is something like that of the solitary. But there is quite a difference in their tone: The song of the yellow-throated is slower and deeper, almost gruff in its effect, but not unpleasantly so.

The song of the white-eyed vireo is in a class by itself. It tends to be louder and more abrupt than those of the others. It usually starts and ends with a sharply pronounced "chick." This "chick-peroweo-chick," often mixed in with a jumble of notes like those heard from catbirds, flickers, and others, makes one think that the singer is right over there in those thick bushes, near at hand. It is astonishing, however, how hard it is to get a good look at him. Just when you think you have him cornered, you find that he has moved to another bush, some distance away. And he often changes his location without your being able to see him go.

All five vireos add considerable charm to the summer, very largely by their notes, even though seeing them requires a good deal of patience.

The
Ruby-Throated
Hummingbird

Sept 28 – Sharp-shinned hawks, kestrels, broadwings, and an occasional bald eagle migrating along Kittatinny mountains all day — near the brushy ground a tiny ruby-throat appeared for an instant by our feet, then was gone....

across the miles to the Gulf of Mexico & Central America — alone! Saw tiny monarch butterflies and darning needles on these aerial highways too.

Hummingbirds have been found only in the Western Hemisphere and mainly in the tropics. So far, some 320 different species have been identified, and they are of all shapes, colors, and sizes—up to about 8 inches and as small as less than 3 inches. A few are found in the Western and Southern parts of the United States, but only one has been willing to brave the more Northern and Eastern climates of this country: the ruby-throated hummingbird. However, he leaves little to complain about, for he is a beautiful and dainty little mite of a bird, a good representative of his exotic species.

The male ruby-throat has, as his name implies, a fiery red throat, which is not shared by his mate. Both sexes have greenish backs and heads, with grayish-white underparts. They are only about 3 inches long, and thus are among the smallest of the birds.

What most distinguishes the hummingbird is the way he flies. With rapidly beating wings, which move so rapidly that they look only like a blur, he can hover; fly backward, down, or up; or dart ahead so fast that you can hardly see him go. As he manuevers, he looks for all the world like a large insect or perhaps a sphinx moth, for which he may be mistaken.

His rapidly beating wings make a humming sound, hence his name. He is also heard, at times, to make a rapid squeaky, chipping sound as he is flying.

There are a number of remarkable things about this little gem. For one thing, as part of his migration southward during the winter, during which he may cover 2,000 miles or more, he may fly 500 miles directly across the Gulf of Mexico, with no time out for eating or resting. No mean feat for a 3-inch midget!

His nest is usually placed on the limb of a tree, 10 feet or so above the ground. It is only about the size of a walnut and is constructed of a delicate combination of fine grasses, moss, lichens, plant down, and even spider webs. Usually there are two pure white eggs, each about the size of a pea.

The "hummer" feeds on small insects and on the nectar of flowers, which he fertilizes in the process, just like bees do. His long bill is well adapted for reaching into flowers.

He appears not at all averse to being near humans; in fact, he often seems to ignore us, and he is glad to come to any of the various tube feeders frequently used to entice him, when they are filled with a sugary fluid.

It was noted that the ruby-throat appeares to have little fear of man. More than that, he hardly seems to know the meaning of fear under any circumstances, and he is just plain pugnacious at times, especially near his nest. It is reported that he has even gone after a hawk when the latter was annoying him for some reason. One wonders how the poor hawk could tell how to "have at" his assailant, not only because of the hummer's size, but also because one never can be sure just where he will be next, so fast and unpredictable are his aerial maneuvers.

May 9 —

In the hushed spring
woods a single bird starts
the concert with a note
or two. Soon others
join in the woodland
chorus until as sunrise
approaches the music
is beyond words — a
hermit thrush sings
his silky melody
just for me —
don't even need to
buy tickets for
this performance.

ts dawn, 5 AM — .
Birdsong is beginning — .

Frequently
wags
russet
tail.

♂

Carol Decker

Many people, including the author, think that the hermit thrush is the finest musician of North American birds. To make sure that this statement does not appear to reflect the opinion of just one person, a few quotations are in order.

John Burroughs once said that the song of the hermit thrush suggests "a serene religious beatitude as no other sound in nature does."[21] And in his book *Wake Robin* he commented further, "Listening to this strain on the lone mountain, . . . the pomp of your cities and the pride of your civilization seemed trivial and cheap."[22]

In *Birds of America,* George Gladden called the hermit thrush the ". . . singer of the purest natural melody to be heard in this or, perhaps, any other land." And, again, he speaks of ". . . the matchless beauty of the song."[23]

And in the National Geographic Society's *Song and Garden Birds of North America,* the following is noted in the article on the hermit thrush:

> Clear and flute like, the haunting music of the hermit thrush floats through the twilight—a serene benediction to the wilderness sunset. One after another the beautiful notes ring out. . . . The sweetest singer of his [the thrush] family, the hermit thrush is often called the American nightingale.[24]

It seems that nothing need be added save by you, after you get to know the song of the hermit thrush. It definitely is worth doing.

However, another comment may be added in description of the hermit's matchless song. It is composed of a series of phrases, each beginning with what may be called an introductory tone note. Each of these pure tone notes is followed, after a brief pause, by a wavering cadence of song at a higher pitch, until that particular phrase is completed. After a pause, another phrase begins, again starting with a tone note, which may be higher or lower than the preceding one, and, again, it is followed by a series of wavering higher notes. Occasionally he also adds a short rather harsh nasal call note sounding something like "pay" or "chay."

The hermit's name is quite descriptive of his retiring ways, at least in the summer. He is usually found in the deep woods near his nest, by himself or in the company of his mate, and he usually flies off when you try to approach him. He loses his shyness in a hurry, however, if you play a tape recording of his song near his nest. He then completely changes his character, diving at the tape recorder with fluffed-up feathers, obviously trying to drive away his competitor and to express his unhappiness over the situation.

In the winter he seems to object less to man's company. While he migrates to a considerable extent, he still is occasionally seen around New Jersey at Christmas time, the only thrush to be so found. He then may sometimes be seen out of the wind on a sheltered porch. He has also been heard to sing, though rarely, during the winter in the southern part of his range.

The hermit thrush is slightly larger than most sparrows. He has an olive-brown back, with white underparts, speckled with black spots, which are somewhat smaller and less conspicuous than those of the wood thrush, which is seen and heard much more often near human habitations during the summer. A distinguishing characteristic of the hermit thrush is his reddish tail, which he frequently raises and lowers while he is perching.

You will not find it easy to get to know the hermit thrush. However, you will find it definitely worth the effort, especially if you appreciate lovely music.

The
Common
Yellowthroat

July 2 —
Little masked
man with a big voice —
Yellowthroat took up residence
near edge of field where it's wet
under foot. No matter
how often I've
looked for
his nest I
haven't found
one yet !

witchery witchery witchery witchery

Carol Decker

The yellowthroat, a member of the warbler family, is found nesting throughout the East during the summer. He is quite shy, generally tending to avoid the vicinity of houses, and is usually hard to approach. But his song rings out clearly and unmistakably at any time during the day.

In contrast to the notes of most birds, the yellowthroat's song may be expressed in our language quite accurately by the phrases "witchery-witchery-witchery-witch." The number of syllables and the placing of the accent frequently vary with the locality. For example, in some places the accent is placed on the first syllable of "witchery"; in others it is placed on the second syllable; in other localities the third syllable may be omitted; and so on. However, it is so unlike the song of any other bird in length, quality, and timing that it is easily recognized after it has been identified only a few times. The yellowthroat also has a rather brief flight song he utters occasionally. This is a sputtering and confused effort as he flies a few feet into the air from his perch, and it may also contain brief snatches of his usual "witchery" song.

Another thing that clearly distinguishes the yellowthroat from other birds is the black mask of the male, which covers much of his forehead and a good deal of his cheeks. This mask has led to his being called by some the *robber bird*. His back is generally olive-brown, his throat and breast bright yellow, and his belly white. His mate is similarly colored, except for the fact that she lacks the black mask.

The yellowthroat, in contrast to many other warblers, tends to spend most of his time near the ground rather than in the tree tops. This would make him easier to see, except for his shy and retiring nature. He is an expert at playing hide-and-seek when you try to approach him. Yet, at times, he may easily be seen as he sings away from the top of a bush.

His favorite habitat also differs from most other warblers in that he seems to prefer swampy and bushy areas, where his nest is usually located. Unfortunately, yellowthroats are quite often hoodwinked by that despicable character, the cowbird, which lays her eggs in the nests of other birds when they are away from them. The unsuspecting parents may then incubate the cowbird's eggs along with their own. When hatched, the young cowbirds may seize all the food the parents bring to the nest, so that the yellowthroats' own young may then die of starvation.

The Yellow-Breasted Chat

June 9 —
Saw the noisy
chat today flying off
through the bushes, feet
dangling, reminding me of
a clumsy teenager —
usually only hear
him squawking.

← Bright
yellow
breast

Carol Decker

The chat, classed as a member of the warbler family, does a great deal to liven up the world about him by his notes and calls, as well as by his behavior. If any bird earns the title of clown, it is he.

The sexes are similar in appearance. Their backs are olive-green in color, their throats and breasts bright yellow, and their underparts are white. They have white spectacles, which stand out against the olive-green of their heads. They are about 7 inches long, quite large for a warbler. They look very much like enlarged versions of the common yellowthroat, except that they lack the male yellowthroat's black mask.

The chat usually first starts to attract our attention by his notes and whistles, which are among the most unusual in the bird world. These vary from loud to soft and from harsh to sweet. John Burroughs, in his book entitled *Wake Robin,* attempted to describe the sounds the chat makes as follows:

> C-r-r-r-r,—whrr,—that's it,—chee,—quack, cluck,—yit-yit-yit,—now hit it,—t-r-r-r,—when, caw, caw,—cut, cut,—tea-boy,—who, who,—mew, mew,—and so on, till you are tired of listening.[25]

While all this is going on, you may be unable to see the source of all the commotion, except, perhaps, for a brief flash of yellow or white through the thick foliage where he likes to hide. And the more you poke around in your attempts to see him, the more he seems to be thoroughly concealed somewhere else. Like some other birds with similar secretive behavior, however, he is very curious and may often be best seen as he peeks stealthily at you from behind the leaves if you remain motionless. If this does not work, you may still identify him without question by the strange sounds he makes, once you get to know them.

In the rare glimpses you may have of him, you will be struck by his clownish behavior. He often sings as he flies, pumping his tail, with his head down, and his feet dangling, in awkward, most unbirdlike fashion. At times he almost seems to be coming apart as he flies. He also has a courtship flight song which he delivers as he flies straight up or hovers with his legs dangling awkwardly. To add to his unusual behavior, he often sings at night as well as by day, especially on moonlit nights.

The chat spends the winter well to our south, but, unlike many members of the warbler family, he is to be found nesting over a wide area of the Eastern states during the summer months. He generally stays aloof from human habitations, preferring to do his clownish acts and to deliver his astonishing vocal performances in the thick vine-covered bushes, alone or with his mate and young.

The Yellow Warbler

Brought green inch worm to youngsters

Carol Decker

♂

June 28 — yellow warbler making trip after trip to feed the kids out of the nest. After delivering the "goodies" warbler hopped up to a higher branch and burst out with song — then off again to find another meal.

While many warblers pay us only brief visits on their way to their more northern breeding grounds and then again on their way south for the winter, the yellow warbler is one of those (along with the common yellowthroat, the oven bird, the blue-winged warbler, and a few others) found in New Jersey all summer long. Furthermore, since they are quite common and not particularly shy around humans, it should not be hard to identify and get to know them.

To some people they are known as "wild canaries" (as goldfinches are also called) or "summer yellowbirds." The latter name goes very well with the fact that they look all yellow at first glance. It is only on closer scrutiny that one sees the chestnut streaks on the breast of the male in the summer. He loses these in the winter, and the female lacks them all year. The backs of both male and female are olive-yellow, and both have yellow spots on their tails. They are about 5 inches long.

The song of the yellow warbler is very sprightly and cheerful and rings out clearly at any time of the day. One version of his song that is quite common is made up of from seven to nine phrases, rapidly delivered. He seems to be saying something like, "chee-chee-chee-chee-cheta-cheta-chee," falling in tone in the "cheta-cheta" section and rising at the end.

It should be emphasized, however, that great variations are to be heard in the song of the yellow warbler, as in the case of most birds. The same individual may sing different songs from time to time with changing circumstances. Also, different neighboring individuals may have their own variations. Add to this local and regional differences, and the beginner may be excused for being thoroughly confused.

To complicate things further, no human language is a good means of imitating any but a very few bird notes. To learn this, all one needs to do is to read the awkward attempts made in different books about birds (including this one) to express bird notes in English and then to compare these with the real thing.

It is suggested that the most productive approach to learning bird notes is to concentrate on analyzing such things as the loudness or softness, the sweetness or harshness, the pitch or tone, and the timing of the sound made by each bird. Bird records help a good deal with this, but a lot of concentrated listening in the field is also needed. Nevertheless, even the experts are taken aback at hearing something entirely new from time to time.

The yellow warbler seems to prefer spending his time and securing his food in low bushes and gardens and along streams, rather than in the tree tops in the deeper woods, where many other warblers are found.

Cowbirds frequently pick on the yellow warbler in their parasitic attempts to fob off the job of raising their young. Yellow warblers, perhaps more than other small birds, seem to realize that something is wrong after the cowbird has laid her egg in their nest, but they do not seem to be able to take entirely effective measures to protect their young. Cases have been found where warblers have added several stories to their nest after a cowbird has laid an egg in each. But the end result is often that the warblers end up incubating the cowbird's egg and feeding the grabby youngster, while their own young perish.

march 22 —
The car headlights
spotlighted a
woodcock for
an instant as it
flew across a road —
It was like a
photo flash forever
recorded in my
mind.

When the calendar indicates that spring is with us, one looks with faith and hope, in spite of the vagaries of the weather, for signs that it is really that time of year again.

Snow drops and crocuses provide support for that faith; but one of the earliest signs of spring—and a real thriller at that—is not generally noticed: the musical, aerial courtship acrobatics of the woodcock.

Usually the woodcock is seen and heard when he suddenly jumps up from practically under our feet as we walk across a brush-filled field, scaring us half to death as he shoots away on whistling wings. But this dumpy, unlikely looking songster really "turns it on" during his spring courtship maneuvers.

The woodcock usually starts his courtship songs during the blustery days of March, and his phenomenal performance may continue well into May. At about dusk in early to mid-March (in some years only on a few evenings and sometimes during the early light of dawn, as well), a nasal "bzeep" coming from some distance away on the ground can be heard by the careful listener. This sounds somewhat like the note of the night hawk as he flies overhead. After a number of these "bzeeps," which come at quite regular intervals of several seconds apart, they suddenly stop. Then, after a short pause, the quavering trill of rapidly beating wings is heard as the bird heads skyward. Sometimes he (it is the male) may be seen in the glimmering light, rapidly flying about as he ascends. Then comes the climax: a faint chipping and chirping, well overhead, lasting for several seconds. Soon that stops, and the bird plummets abruptly and silently to the ground. The "bzeeps" then start up again, to be followed by another round of the same musical acrobatics overhead; and so on for some time into the growing darkness.

The male's objectives, naturalists believe, are two in number: to attract a mate and to stake out his territorial claims against any rivals.

However long this show may last, its beginning is one of the surest and most exciting harbingers of spring. In *A Naturalist Buys an Old Farm*, Edwin Way Teale wrote about it as ". . . . the magical flight song of the woodcock," and as ". . . one of the most profoundly moving events in the life of our meadows."[26]

The Common Loon

November 15 —
Two loons today
migrating along
mountain ridge —
Loons winter on
our larger lakes —
usually see
one at
Christmas
time.

carol Deckerd

winter
plumage

To this observer, there are two especially noteworthy things about the common loon: first, his calls, which are described in a number of ways, rarely in less than superlatives; and, second, his phenomenal ability to dive and swim under water for long times and distances. In fact, one of his common names is the "great northern diver."

His calls seem to remind one of the north woods, with their clear, deep lakes, probably because that is where he generally is heard. Two types of calls make up most of his repertoire. Of these, one is a long, drawn-out three-syllabled lugubrious wail, which may be heard for long distances over the surface of a lake on a calm night. A number of attempts have been made to imitate this call by using our alphabet and language, but these are far from successful. One may get a feel for its melody and timing by going to the piano and striking the "E," two notes above middle "C," and holding it briefly; then striking the "B," four notes above the "E," and holding it twice as long; then returning to the original "E," and holding it briefly again. Finally, whistle that same melody, with the timing as indicated.

This call attains to depths of melancholy almost as low as we humans would seem to deserve, considering the way we often behave toward one another. His other main call sounds like loud hysterical laughter, in which he may be expressing his feeling about the meaning of it all. These two calls, by way of comparison, almost make the mourning dove sound like an optimist.

The loon's ability to dive from the surface of the

water and to stay under for a long time may be the source of considerable fun. Try chasing him in a canoe, when the next opportunity comes along, perhaps placing bets on how long he will stay under and where he will come up next. When just feeding, he may stay under for a half minute or so. But, when he feels he is being pursued, he seems to stay under for ages. His dives, then, may last up to three or maybe even five minutes, and you can never be sure which way to look for him to come up. He may swim several hundred yards under water. Is he having fun too?

The loon is a poor performer on land, shuffling along awkwardly and with difficulty. His (and her) nest, consequently, is located not far from the water's edge, generally on the ground, perhaps on a secluded island or point on a lake, where the parents can get back into their natural element in a hurry. The loon also has difficulty rising into the air from the surface of the water, and does so only after much thrashing of wings and feet. Once he makes it, he flies strongly and fast, with rapid wing beats, holding his head low, his large feet sticking out behind his tail.

The common loon is half again as big as a crow. He has a long, black, dagger-like bill, which he uses for spearing crustaceans and fish, his principal food. He has large webbed feet, used to good advantage as he swims. His color is generally dark above and white below. In the summer his back and neck become spotted with white. The sexes are alike.

After spending the summers on the lakes of the north woods, they migrate south for various distances, mainly along the coast, before returning to their summer quarters again.

The Great Horned Owl

October 29 —
Disturbed great
horned owl
hidden in
daytime
roost among
dark hemlocks —

Carol Decker

...t in
...e open songbirds gather
...o mob & harass the owl
...who leaves knowing
he'll get no further rest
here.

Anyone who has heard a great horned owl sound off in the middle of the night can understand at least part of the meaning of the word *awesome*. Assuming that the listener has the normal touch of the superstitious in his or her makeup, he or she might have even felt a cold chill running up and down the spine at the sound. In the emotions of the ancients (as well as some moderns), owls are said to have been associated with witches and the other powers of darkness. There is among many the conviction that, wherever found, owls are an evil omen.

While other notes and calls may be heard from the great horned owl (including hideous screeches from the young when they are hungry), his usual call is five or six deep hoots. The one I heard the other night timed his six hoots as follows: "hoo—hoo-hoo-hoo—hoo–hoo-." By way of contrast, the barrel owl, also heard at night in these parts, usually gives about eight hoots, the timing and inflection of which have been expressed as: "Who cooks for you—who cooks for you-all?"

One hot, sunny afternoon a summer or so ago, I was sitting alone, feeling somewhat dejected, on the bank of a trout stream in the Pocono mountains. Why wouldn't those pesky trout fall for my fly, and what could I do about it? Suddenly, out of the corner of my eye, I saw a movement, and the next thing I knew a great horned owl landed without a sound in a tree on the opposite side of the stream. His size was startling—about 2 feet long—and he had a tremendous wing spread—perhaps 5 feet of it! He was a streaked and mottled mixture of brown and white. He sat with his "horns" up, moving his head from side to side, apparently to get a better look at me. His yellow eyes—I can feel them still—seemed to have a glint of deep malevolence in them as he took me in, although I suppose he was merely curious about the strange creature sitting so quietly on the opposite bank. After he had apparently satisfied his curiosity and decided that I was not edible, he took off, silently again, up the stream.

The term *tiger of the air* seems particularly appropriate as a means of describing the great horned owl and his doings. The results of his swift and silent swoop are usually fatal to his prey, which varies from insects, fish, frogs, snakes, and birds all the way to mammals of many kinds. Woe betide the mouse, rat, squirrel, rabbit, and even the ground hog and skunk (the owl's sense of smell is thought not to be acute) which comes within the range of his keen eyes and ears and powerful talons! He is easily persuaded to a chicken diet if these are left unprotected. He has even been known to tangle (not always successfully) with house cats and porcupines.

In defense of his or her young, the owl's ferocity appears to know no bounds. Several cases have been reported of curious humans who, having climbed a tree to get a good, close look at the nest of one of these owls, have suffered severely as a result. Not only have they had their hats knocked off, but some have also taken with them deep scars on their arms, sides, and scalps from the birds' talons.

These owls are not the tidiest of housekeepers. Often appropriating the nests of other owls or hawks, the nests usually become filthy and malodorous with bones, other remains of the owl's prey, and offal scattered all over the place.

To prove their hardiness, great horned owls are among the first birds to nest in our area in the early spring, sometimes as early as January or February. Cases are known of their being found incubating their eggs with a thick blanket of snow on their backs.

While not the most attractive of playmates, the great horned owl is surely among the most interesting of all the birds.

July 28—
Brown pelican
flying over the
coast — visit here
occasionally
from the
south.

Anyone at all observant of the outdoor scene along our Southern coasts and brackish bays cannot fail to have been struck by the contradictory impressions received from watching the brown pelicans: waddling about awkwardly and gawkily when they move about on land, but flying gracefully, majestically, and even magnificently in the air.

The size of the pelican contributes a good deal to these contrasting impressions—he may be over 4 feet long, with a wingspread of 6 feet or more. His floppy wings along with his huge bill and bulky pouch look unwieldy on land; but they are held and used in a dignified manner as he flies or dives.

Brown pelicans vary a good deal in color from summer to winter and as they mature. The bills are gray, and the backs and underparts are generally various shades of gray and brown all year long, but the heads and necks show different shades of brown, white, and even yellow (on the front of the heads of the adults). They have webs between their toes, which enable them to swim strongly.

They make few sounds, except for grunts and croaks, to the accompaniment of much wing flapping, as they compete impolitely with one another over the remains of fish thrown to them by fisherman as they clean their catch. Pelicans always seem to be on the lookout for such handouts. They gather together in large numbers at such times, seeming to lose most of their fear of humans in the excitement of the feast.

At the ocean front, an entirely different sort of pelican show takes place. First, there approaches a long, fairly regularly spaced line of the great birds flying a considerable distance above the water, with their pouches and giant bills resting unobtrusively against their breasts. They glide majestically for a while, then flap their wings slowly and deliberately, and then glide again. In shifting from gliding to wing flapping and back to gliding again, they often appear to be following the example of the leading bird, but not always. Sometimes individuals in the line go their own way in this matter.

But now comes an even more spectacular sight. Barely clearing the tops of waves, another line of pelicans comes into view. Often, it appears, they are about to be engulfed by a big comber. Yet, they fly along with what seems to be the utmost confidence, right through the troughs between the waves, with never a feather getting wet. As they follow this considerably less roomy flight path, again, wing flapping and gliding are alternated. As before, one is tempted to conclude that the leading bird decides just when they should glide and when they should flap their wings and passes the word back to the others through his example, but it does not always work out that way.

Another part of the show is still to come. A lone pelican is flying 60 or 70 feet above the water. Suddenly we see him close his wings and dive beak first into the water after a fish, landing with a terrific splash. If he is successful, he comes up with a fish in his capacious pouch, which he has thus used as a dip net. Along with the fish comes a lot of salt water, perhaps 3½ gallons of it. He pauses on the surface to drain off the water and swallow the fish, unless some enterprising gull manages to steal the fish while the water is being drained out, which sometimes happens.

The brown pelican is a sociable bird. Not only is he willing to be near humans (especially those cleaning fish), but he is also generally seen with or near his own kind, either as he flies or as he roosts at night. In Florida he often spends the night in large flocks, one pelican perching on about every available spot on the branches of the trees, reminding one of Christmas trees overcrowded with decorations.

The white pelican, a mostly Western relative of the brown pelican, is also found along the shores of southern Florida, for example, near Flamingo in the Everglades. He is a good deal larger than the brown pelican, being 5 feet or more long, with a wingspread of up to 8 or 9 feet. He is mostly pure white, except for black on the back part of his wings. The adults also have a large yellow bill. Unlike the brown pelican, he does not dive for fish, but scoops them up with his bill as he swims on the surface, often teaming up with others of his kind to round up the fish and drive them close to shore where they may more easily be seized.

September 11 —

Banding hawks on top of the mountain during southern autumn hawk migration — vultures overhead.

grey head →

adults have red heads.

Carol Decker

Suddenly two young turkey vultures tried to attack the pigeon being used to lure hawks to fly into mist nets. Vultures acting more like predators than scavengers!

The turkey vulture certainly would not win any beauty contest! His costume is a rather dingy and unkempt mixture of brownish and black feathers. Add to this his bare reddish head, and his appearance is just plain ugly.

The feeding habits of vultures are also unglamorous, to say the least. They generally feed on the carcasses of animals that have died in the fields or been killed along the roads by passing cars. They are far from fastidious as they squabble with one another over these remains.

However, before we write off the turkey vulture as an undesirable member of the community, let us not forget that he makes an important contribution toward keeping the environment clean—by doing away with carrion. Surely none of us would want to change jobs with him.

Vultures are less than graceful as they walk and hop around on the ground. Also, they appear awkward as they try to get off the ground. But once they succeed in taking off, they soon prove themselves masters of the air currents. Their great wings, often 6 feet across, are of two tones, gray and black. With these held in a shallow V-shape, they are able to mount hundreds of feet on the air currents and to soar aloft for hours, tilting from side to side, needing only rarely to flap their wings.

When they are soaring close enough to the ground, one may see their reddish heads moving about as they scan the ground for their next meal. Their eyesight is so keen that they can spot dead animals from considerable heights. After one vulture alights, generally he is joined before long by others who have soared in from practically beyond human eyesight to partake of the feast.

Turkey vultures migrate north and south to some extent, usually returning to their cleanup jobs with us in early April. In the southern part of their range, they mix with their southern cousins—the black vultures. The black vulture can be distinguished from the turkey vulture by his smaller size; he also has white spots near his wing tips; and he appears less adept at using the air currents, flapping his wings more often than the turkey vulture.

Turkey vultures appear much less particular than other birds about where they make their nests. Their eggs may be laid in caves or in rock crevices, sometimes in hollow logs, and even occasionally on the bare ground.

About the only sounds to be heard from the turkey vulture are hisses and grunts as he feeds, and these do not seem at all inappropriate, considering the things he eats.

To sum up, on the ground the turkey vulture appears to be one of the least favored of all the birds. His looks, his behavior, and his sounds are unattractive to humans, to put it mildly. However, he quickly wins our admiration as we watch him soar with great skill through the heavens. But he should really win kudos for the job he does for all of us as a scavenger—in helping to keep the environment clean. Because of this, he is protected by law in many parts of the United States. The Environmental Protection Agency has in him a real ally.

The
Osprey

April 21 — Fish hawk lifted off river with fish it just caught. Carried prey head first in straight line with its own body and holding with both feet. Two crows harass and dive at it. Osprey left tree it had landed in carrying fish same way to escape crows — Fish looks like a shad.

Carol Decker

Roger Tory Peterson, in an article he wrote on the osprey in the 1965 National Geographic Society's *Water, Prey, and Game Birds of North America,* commented that it was a status symbol to have an osprey's nest near one's house in the community in which he moved in 1954—Old Lyme, near the mouth of the Connecticut River.[27] He went on to note that there had been a serious decline in the osprey population since he moved there, the number of nests dropping from 150 in 1954 to 17 by 1964. This he attributed to the increased use of insecticides in the area, which made their way through the food chain to harm the ospreys. The same decline has been noted in a number of other localities, and attempts are being made to counteract it by releasing young and vigorous birds in localities where the water is relatively free of pollution.

The nests of ospreys are truly monumental in size and often increase in dimensions each year as the birds continue to use them, building them larger each season until they become among the biggest of all bird nests.

Some of these nests have been used and been added to for forty years. In building them up, the birds accumulate all sorts of debris, which has included limbs of trees, rubber boots, axe handles, fish nets, rag dolls, tops of trash cans—almost anything available and movable. As these structures have grown in size, various smaller birds have made their nests in the spaces between the debris, thus becoming "basement tenants" in the structure. Their presence apparently is not resented by the landlords, who, however, are extremely aggressive in defending their nest and young against threats of harm, from whatever source.

These nests, of course, are not hard to find. They are usually placed on top of some big, dead tree or on telephone or power poles. This has sometimes led to complications, for as the junk from which the structure is built becomes wet from the rains, short circuits have developed. Some enterprising power companies have attempted to circumvent this difficulty by putting up bases for osprey nests in places where they will do no harm.

The osprey presents a magnificent spectacle as he flaps his wings in slow, deep, and rather labored fashion overhead, soaring occasionally. He is usually about 2 feet long, with a wing spread of 5 feet or more. He is generally dark above and white below, with a broad pitch of black along the side of his white head. Also observable are black "wrists" at the crook of his wings. In contrast, his calls are usually a relatively undistinguished but sharp "cheep, cheep, cheep," although other calls are occasionally heard from him.

The osprey feeds mainly on fish and for this reason is also called the *fish hawk,* and a master fisherman he is. He is generally found along seacoasts or on lakes or rivers, migrating with the seasons and with the movements of his food supply. His fishing procedure is spectacular to watch. After hovering to locate his prey some 50 to 100 feet above the water, he suddenly dives, feet first, with a great splash, often going under the surface briefly to sink his sharp talons into the fish. He has rough projections on the under surfaces of his toes, which, along with his talons, help him to hold on to his slippery prey. In fact, he apparently has such difficulty letting go that he is sometimes drowned when he attaches himself to a fish too big for him to handle. In a number of cases, an osprey's skeleton has been found attached to a large fish caught in a net.

Generally, however, he manages to fly off with his catch, which he shares with his mate and young. His plans are occasionally foiled by a bald eagle, which pursues the osprey, often forcing him to release his fish, which the eagle then seizes for his own purposes.

march 18 — Marsh hawk hunting low
over field after thaw.   Pounces on
grass nests or clumps — the kind made by
field mice tunneling under snow —
lifts each clump of grass
then drops it and
on to another —

white
rump
feathers →

Perhaps
in the past
these pounces
have revealed
a running mouse
to a
hungry
hawk.

Brown
color, perhaps ♀
or immature .

Probably have !

Carol Decker

The marsh hawk (also called the *northern harrier*) is one of the hawks most easily identified by the amateur birder. Many hawks usually fly so high that it is hard to distinguish their specific characteristics, or they are found in wooded country, where they are not easily seen. The marsh hawk, on the other hand, generally flies close to the ground and over open country, where it may readily be observed. Furthermore, its conspicuous white rump stands out as a good means of identification. The plumage of the adult male is generally a light gray, whereas that of the female is brownish; but the white rump stands out clearly on both.

The marsh hawk is usually seen gliding gracefully a few feet above the ground, methodically patrolling the marshes, grasslands, or meadows in search of his next meal. The wings are held in a shallow V-shape, as in the case of the turkey vulture. Occasionally he stops suddenly, hovers briefly, and then dives after his prey. Marsh hawks, unlike other hawks, are rarely seen perching on trees; and they are said to roost on the ground at night.

Their diet varies with the different times of year, but consists mostly of rodents, with field mice appearing to be their particular favorites. They also eat insects, snakes, and frogs, as well as birds and chickens, when these are available. They migrate north and south with the seasons, presumably influenced by the available food supply.

The usual call of the marsh hawk is a rather weak but sharp series of nasal whistles, hard to describe, but unmistakable once heard.

Males of many species do all sorts of queer things to attract mates, but the courtship antics of the marsh hawk pretty nearly tops those of all other birds. His flight during these maneuvers has been compared to the course of a bouncing ball, as he follows a pattern which looks like a series of U-shapes. At the top of each U, he stalls briefly before starting down on the next one, diving gracefully to within a few feet of the ground before starting the next upswing. The average number of U's in each series is said to be about twenty-five. Some claim that he closes his wings and does somersaults at various stages of his performance. (Does this not remind you of Tom Sawyer's showing off before Becky Thatcher?) Sometimes the female appears inspired enough to join the male in these antics. And when the female is on the ground, the male walks at her side bowing and scraping like the most solicitous of courtiers.

The nests are usually built on or near the ground and are constructed mostly by the females, with the males bringing in some sticks to help out. She, however, apparently reserves the right to decide what will go where in the building process.

Marsh hawks aggressively defend their nests and young. They appear fearlessly intolerant of any intruders anywhere near their young. They attack and drive away crows and other smaller birds, as well as other hawks and even eagles. One writer described how the parent birds repeatedly dove at his head, just missing him by inches, as he approached their nest. Another was struck on the head a number of times, and his hat was knocked off as he tried to set up a tripod for his camera near a nest. Another, also trying to get pictures of a nest, had the bellows of his camera torn apart.

All of these investigators clearly came up against an ancient and powerful instinct—one shared by many living things (including humans)—the instinct that dictates that personal safety comes second when the safety of their young appears threatened in any way.

The Sparrow Hawk

December 11 —
Trying to drive
near kestrel sitting on
top of telephone pole — when
too close he looks down and
takes off to land
on next pole —
Did this pole
hopping trick twice.
You win hawk! Too
many poles down
the road
ahead —

Carol Decker S

The sparrow hawk (also called the *American kestrel*) is probably the most sociable of all the birds of prey, as far as humans are concerned. While most hawks seem anxious to keep a good distance from us, the sparrow hawk appears willing to live and hunt nearby, and it is often seen perched on wires and trees near houses. It may also be tamed and trained for falconry.

Since he does not seem to mind being fairly near us and is quite commonly seen, we are able to study and get to know the sparrow hawk rather easily, especially since he has a number of distinctive characteristics.

Sparrow hawks are the smallest of the hawks along the Eastern Seaboard, being only slightly larger than a robin. Their plumage is striking and beautiful: The back and tail of both sexes are a rather bright reddish-brown, which flashes for all to see as they fly about. Another striking feature of the plumage of both males and females are the sideburn-like streaks of black against the white sides of their heads. Both sexes also have a chestnut-colored crown. The males have bluish wings, whereas the wings of the females are brown, the same color as their backs.

Their distinctive behavior also helps to identify sparrow hawks. One of their colloquial names is *windhover,* which is descriptive of the way they hover for minutes at a time on rapidly beating wings (much like a kingfisher) while trying to locate their prey. Their eyesight is said to be especially keen, one student estimating that it is nine times keener than that of a human. They also share a habit with many other birds—for example, with phoebes, catbirds, hermit thrushes, mockingbirds, palm warblers, and so on—of raising and lowering their tails occasionally as they perch on a wire or the branch of a tree. (Why do some birds, but not others, do this? Just another of the many unsolved mysteries of the world of nature!)

Any further question about the sparrow hawk's identity is removed as soon as we hear his rapid, strident, and authoritative call of "killy-killy-killy."

Sparrow hawks, during the warm months, feed on caterpillars, crickets, and grasshoppers. They also occasionally prey on small birds or young chickens, although the word *sparrow* in their name overemphasizes that part of their diet. During most of the year they prey on small mammals, especially mice. They migrate to some extent with the seasons.

The sparrow hawk usually lays her eggs deep into all sorts of available holes: natural cavities in trees, woodpecker holes, rock cavities, holes in banks, or cavities she finds in outbuildings, as well as birdhouses. Unlike many birds, little or no nesting material is added by the parents, the eggs being deposited either on the bare floor of the hole or on whatever else was there before, which may include droppings of previous occupants, and bits of trash of various sorts.

As one gets to know the sparrow hawk, one finds him to be strikingly beautiful, generally beneficial in what he feeds on, and interesting and good company (unless one happens to be a mouse or a grasshopper).

Notes

1. Walt Whitman, "Specimen Days: Birds—and a Caution," *Walt Whitman,* selected and with notes by Mark Van Doren (New York: The Viking Press, 1945) p. 678.

2. Carl Bode, *The Best of Thoreau's Journals* (Carbondale, Ill.: Southern Illinois University Press, 1971) p. 11.

3. Edwin Way Teal, *Wandering Through Winter* (New York: Dodd, Mead & Company, Inc., 1981) pp. 83–84.

4. Roger Tory Peterson, *A Field Guide to the Birds East of the Rockies,* 4th ed., (Boston: Houghton Mifflin Company, 1980) p. 223.

5. E. M. Betts, "Preface," in Thomas Jefferson, *Thomas Jefferson's Garden Book* (Philadelphia: American Philosophical Society, 1944) pp. v–vi.

6. Ibid., p. xv.

7. George Washington, quoted in Paul L. Haworth, *George Washington* (Indianapolis, Ind.: The Bobb Merrill Co., Inc., 1925) p. 2.

8. Paul L. Haworth, *George Washington,* p. 77.

9. Roger Tory Peterson, *A Field Guide to the Birds.*

10. *Edwin Way Teale, North with the Spring* (New York: Dodd, Mead & Company, 1981) p. 40.

11. Lewis Thomas, *The Lives of a Cell* (New York: Bantam Books, Inc., 1975) p. 22.

12. John K. Terres, *The Audubon Society Encyclopedia of North American Birds* (New York: Alfred A. Knopf, Inc., 1980) p. 919.

13. James Whitcomb Riley, *James Whitcomb Riley's Complete Works* (Indianapolis, Ind.: The Bobbs Merrill Co., Inc., 1913) p. 1123.

14. John Burroughs, as quoted in *Birds of America* (Garden City, N.Y.: Garden City Publishing Company, Inc., 1936) p. 178.

15. William Shakespeare, *Romeo and Juliet,* act 1, sc. 2, lines 86–87.

16. William Shakespeare, *Macbeth,* act 3, sc. 2, lines 47–52.

17. William Shakespeare, *The Merchant of Venice,* act 5, sc. 1, lines 102–103.

18. Edwin Way Teale, *A Naturalist Buys an Old Farm* (New York: Dodd, Mead & Company, 1974) p. 160.

19. As noted in Arthur Cleveland Bent, *Life Histories of North American American Nuthatches, Wrens, Thrashers and Their Allies,* Smithsonian Institution Bulletin 195 (Washington, D.C.: U.S. Government Printing Office, 1948) pp. 114–115.

20. John Kieran, *An Introduction to Birds* (Garden City, N.Y.: Garden City Books, 1946) p. 7.

21. John Burroughs, as quoted in *Birds of America,* p. 235.

22. John Burroughs, *Wake Robin* (Boston: Houghton Mifflin and Company, 1885) p. 66.

23. George Gladden, as quoted in *Birds of America,* pp. 234–235.

24. From an article by E. Thomas Gilliard in *Song and Garden Birds of North America* by Alexander Wetmore and other eminent ornithologists (Washington, D.C.: National Geographic Society, 1964) p. 216.

25. Burroughs, *Wake Robin,* p. 200.

26. Teale, *A Naturalist,* pp. 51–52.

27. From an article by Roger Tory Peterson in *Water, Prey, and Game Birds of North America* by Alexander Wetmore and other eminent ornithologists (Washington, D.C.: National Geographic Society, 1965) p. 248.

Brief ——
Annotated
Bibliography

KIERAN, JOHN, *An Introduction to Birds*. Garden City, New York: Garden City Books, 1946.

> An excellent book for the beginner. Relaxed, informative, and very well-written discussion of many of our most common birds, with color pictures of each.

PEARSON, T. G., *Birds of America*. Garden City, New York: Garden City Publishing, 1936.

> Gives wide coverage with many pictures. Featured by brief, personally signed articles about the various species by a number of distinguished ornithologists.

PETERSON, ROGER TORY, *A Field Guide to the Birds East of the Rockies* (4th ed.). Boston: Houghton Mifflin, 1980.

> The "Second Bible" for birders. Featured by lines drawn to distinguishing marks in color picture of each species, which greatly helps in the identification of the birds. On page opposite these pictures is a brief description of each bird.

REILLY, EDGAR M., JR., *The Audubon Illustrated Handbook of American Birds*. New York: McGraw-Hill, 1968.

> Very complete coverage with mostly black-and-white pictures. Discussion of each species following comments about its group. Not intended as a guide but as a reference book.

ROBBINS, CHANDLER S., BERTEL BRUUN, AND HERBERT S. ZIM, *A Guide to Field Identification. Birds of North America*. New York: Golden Press, 1966.

> A good companion to Peterson's bird guides. An especially helpful feature is that the range of each species is shown next to a brief description of that bird. The picture of each bird is on the page opposite the description.

BRIEF ANNOTATED BIBLIOGRAPHY

TERRES, JOHN K., *The Audubon Society Encyclopedia of North American Birds*. New York: Knopf, 1980.

A monumental work, over 1,000 pages. Many facts with extensive cross-referencing. Lovely pictures of the birds, along with their descriptions. Worth a good long look.

WETMORE, ALEXANDER, and other eminent ornithologists, *Song and Garden Birds of North America*. Washington, D.C.: National Geographic Society, 1964.

A comprehensive reference book, with excellent color pictures of each species. A very important addition is a phonograph record of the songs of seventy birds tucked in the back of the book.

——, *Water, Prey, and Game Birds of North America*. Washington, D.C.: National Geographic Society, 1965.

Contains articles by distinguished ornithologists and provides extensive coverage with outstanding color pictures. A good companion book for the author's *Song and Garden Birds of North America*.

Index